Advice to Thrive By

How to Use Your Résumé and Cover Letter to Build Your Brand and Launch a Dynamic Public Interest Career

PORTIA ALLEN-KYLE

ABA
AMERICAN BAR ASSOCIATION
Senior Lawyers Division

Cover design by Elmarie Jara/ABA Design

Printed in the United States of America.

26 25 24 23 22   5 4 3 2 1

Library of Congress Cataloging-in-Publication Data

Names: Allen-Kyle, Portia, author. | American Bar Association. Senior Lawyers Division, sponsoring body.
Title: Advice to thrive by : how to use your résumé and cover letter to build your brand and launch a dynamic public interest career / Portia Allen-Kyle.
Description: Chicago, Illinois : American Bar Association, [2022] | Includes bibliographical references and index. | Summary: "This book demystifies career trajectories for law students and young attorneys pursuing careers in the public interest by providing accessible tips for crafting impactful resumes and cover letters, and a professional development strategy to employ using those materials"--Provided by publisher.
Identifiers: LCCN 2022023114 (print) | LCCN 2022023115 (ebook) | ISBN 9781639051915 (hardcover) | ISBN 9781639051922 (ebook)
Subjects: LCSH: Public interest law--Vocational guidance--United States. | Job hunting--United States. | Applications for positions--United States.
Classification: LCC KF299.P8 A45 2022 (print) | LCC KF299.P8 (ebook) | DDC 340.023/73--dc23/eng/20220801
LC record available at https://lccn.loc.gov/2022023114
LC ebook record available at https://lccn.loc.gov/2022023115

Discounts are available for books ordered in bulk. Special consideration is given to state bars, CLE programs, and other bar-related organizations. Inquire at Book Publishing, ABA Publishing, American Bar Association, 321 N. Clark Street, Chicago, Illinois 60654-7598.

www.shopABA.org

Contents

Preface

I deliberately wrote this book in a style that is conversational and markedly different from the way you will write professional materials such as your résumé and cover letter. The reason for this is simple: I want people to read this book. I am a strong believer that the most useful information is accessible and straightforward. Formal writing, by its very nature, has an air of exclusivity. The purpose of formal writing in the context of a job search is so that a person on the outside (i.e., the applicant) can demonstrate why they are qualified to gain entry into a more exclusive insider club or network (i.e., the target organization). Over the years I have reviewed hundreds of sets of application materials belonging to law students and practicing attorneys alike, often seeking to start their careers in public interest, or to realign their careers with their passions and values. This book is the result of compiling comments and feedback placed into the margins of these résumés and cover letters. Like with those informal reviews, my goal is to demystify this process for law students and young attorneys passionate about working in the public interest not just to obtain one job, but to have a plan to help guide them through professional growth and development to navigate their desired career trajectory.

This book is intended for law students and young attorneys, but the advice that follows may be useful to any attorney with compassion and a personal mission to serve the public interest. While some of the advice in here is new, much of what lies ahead in this book has been passed down by attorneys and law students across the profession. However, such advice is often passed down ad hoc and without context; in some situations, advice that could have been given proactively is provided as feedback after a faux pas or violation of another social norm in the legal field. It is my intention to link all of the various nuggets of advice, both old and new, and to place them in the context of a strategy for professional development to keep you at the top of your game and in the race.

Whereas many structures and practices in the legal profession were meant to keep people out, I hope that this book is a tangible step toward inclusivity in the profession to allow talented, passionate people to become their best selves and achieve the career goals they intend.

1

Introduction

> "Luck is what happens when preparation meets opportunity."
>
> —Seneca, Roman philosopher

I was encouraged to write this short book because I was discouraged. Over the years I have reviewed hundreds of résumés from young law students and recent graduates. While I personally knew many of them to be bright and dynamic with promising futures, all of their résumés either significantly undersold both their experience and potential, lacked focus and specificity, or both. Many of us enter law school with the aspirations of landing a clutch, dream job afterward. As students we spend an obscene number of hours over the course of law school studying to obtain respectable grade point averages (GPAs), followed by hundreds of hours studying for the bar exam in order to pass the test to become licensed. Despite all this, I have seen young attorneys often spend just a few hours combined writing a résumé and cover letter, knowing full well that this is often the first thing potential employers will use to judge them and that their first job can set the course for their career. Worse yet, they write these documents after a quick, often generic, Google search for résumé templates. Some law students don't even rewrite their résumés upon entering the legal profession and just continue adding to the same résumé they wrote as undergraduates. This puts them at even more of a disadvantage, as their original résumés were rarely up to the task. But it is not enough to just write a good résumé. If you are going to excel as a public interest attorney it is best to have a goal for your career and a strategy to achieve it.

> The word résumé is often spelled in different ways. Formally, the word resume is spelled with two accents, one over each "e." In more colloquial contexts it is not uncommon to see it spelled with only one diacritical, or accent, mark over the second "e" (i.e., resumé) or none at all, leaving the reader to infer meaning from context. As you are compiling your materials you should default to formal spellings of the word "resume" using accent marks over both "e's" (i.e., résumé). This may seem pretentious, and that is because caring how many accent marks there are IS pretentious. However, you need to know your audience and, until you do, should default to the formal spelling. After all, your résumé is a piece of formal writing for the express purpose of securing the bag, whether that be a job, fellowship, award, or other professional opportunity. While I would venture to say that most potential employers will not care, there are some guards of the profession who will pass you over and assume you are unqualified because you didn't use the formal spelling. I once came across a then-law clerk (less than two years out of law school) who proudly stated that, when reviewing résumés for her judge, she discarded every résumé from a clerkship applicant that failed to use two accent marks. While this is rare, I encourage you to err on the side of caution as you get to know your audience.

There is no shortage of résumé advice out there, but that is precisely why this guide is so important. The results that a Google search returns are often general, short articles and generic samples mostly inapplicable to fresh attorneys, with many telling you *what* to do, but not *how* to do it. Even the guides that exist specifically for attorneys overemphasize private practice generally, and Big Law in particular, leaving a wide gap in career advice and resources available to aspiring public interest attorneys. This is so despite findings from the 2012 wave of the After the JD survey, a longitudinal study of career trajectories of law school graduates conducted by the American Bar Association, that indicates the private sector is shrinking while the share of attorneys in government, public interest, or nonprofit positions is growing.[1] While there are some common conventions that apply to legal résumés, my goal is to provide young attorneys interested in careers in public interest and advocacy with an approach and framework for professional growth and development using their résumé (and cover letter) to launch their career. Law school and the first few years of practice are a time to gain global competencies and begin to develop substantive expertise. Through my approach, young attorneys will be able to take advantage of this time in their careers to also proactively build their brand and reputation to launch a thriving legal career.

During trying times in law school some of my classmates would often say "C = JD," meaning that even if you don't get that A in Contracts it is not the end of the world and you will still graduate. (People also say "C" for "continue.") There is a time and place for this mindset, but there is a difference between mantras to survive by and mantras to thrive by. While a C average may still allow you to graduate with a juris doctor (JD), having a JD in and of itself does not automatically mean a flourishing career as a respected attorney.

---

[1] American Bar Foundation and The NALP Foundation for Law Career Research and Education, *After the JD III: Third Results from a National Study of Legal Careers (2014),* http://www.americanbarfoundation.org/uploads/cms/documents/ajd3report_final_for_distribution.pdf.

To be sure, I once had a conversation with a group of attorneys where one person shared how their entire career trajectory changed when, after numerous applications, they were rejected from all of the mission-driven legal nonprofit organizations and public defender offices they applied to. The reason they believed they were shut down: They didn't put their best foot forward for the job. They submitted a solid application: a top school, with great grades and experience. They wrote a "legal résumé" and applied with the same cover letter they used to secure their prior summer internships at firms, but on reflection did not think they conveyed why they were passionate and aligned with the mission-driven organizations they were applying to. Whether I was serving on hiring committees, working with clients on equitable hiring practices, or interviewing as a candidate myself, I consistently experienced hiring managers, colleagues, and recruiters alike attempting to filter candidates by using markers of "commitment" or "dedication," often arbitrarily. These markers of commitment to public interest can include law school extracurriculars; prior or current work experience; and cues about race, class, or socioeconomic status. That said, whether a candidate is considered "committed" or a "real" public interest attorney should not be underestimated in terms of obstacles to overcome to get in the door. Thus, a critical aim of this book is to demystify the public interest sector and equip law students and young attorneys with the tools to take their career trajectory into their own hands. This professional development strategy, combined with practical tips for crafting résumés and cover letters, will set law students and young attorneys apart from the pack to secure jobs and launch a successful public interest career.

The strategy itself is rather straightforward and comprises three parts. First, start with yourself. That is, do the necessary combination of introspection and research to outline a clear vision of the future of your career. Second, you need to become the preferred candidate.

This means crafting and executing a strategy to gain the specific substantive and soft skills necessary to be competitive in your next opportunity. Finally, you should use your materials (primarily your résumé and cover letter, but also your LinkedIn profile) to demonstrate the acquisition of these skills through both employment and volunteer or pro bono service each year. Chapter 2 provides an overview of the areas of law practiced by public interest attorneys, as well as the practice settings that they are typically employed in. Chapter 3 details my proposed strategy of professional development, providing tools to develop, tailor, and implement your own strategy to keep you competitive and support achieving your professional goals. Chapter 4 explores how your résumé can serve as a brand ambassador and discusses considerations for brand management and recognition. Chapter 5 includes tips for crafting a compelling narrative of your experience through the sections of your résumé. Chapter 6 discusses the mechanics of résumé writing and provides recommendations on style and format. Chapter 7 covers your complementary materials: the cover letter and LinkedIn profile. Chapter 8 describes phases of the hiring process, while chapter 9 provides advice as to how to stay on brand from post-application until you receive an invitation to interview. Chapter 10 weighs in on what happens after you have an interview lined up, with advice ranging from general tips on preparation to making a good impression and utilizing your references. Chapter 11 encourages readers to consider the role–and limitations–of networking to achieve their career goals. This book concludes with a summary of highlights of the strategy.

I am writing this book as a way to pay it forward. The reality is that the legal profession is steeped in elitism, tradition, and unspoken norms and expectations. Law is also a field where professional branding and reputation can either open doors or cause them to be slammed in your face. This book provides a comprehensive approach to career development by teaching law students and young attorneys to use their résumé and cover letter—key aspects of your professional brand—to guide their career development as a public interest lawyer. By implementing my strategy you can measure your progress against your goal as you fine-tune old skills, acquire new ones, and grow your brand. Taking these steps will keep you competitive in the job market and ready for opportunities to serve the profession, amplify your impact, and further your career.

Over the years I have come across a number of law students who asked me how I obtained certain professional accomplishments. Whether I am going for a new job, applying for a fellowship, or looking to join a board, I often know what it takes to not only get in the door, but obtain that position. The open secret is to know, and be, the ideal candidate. As expected, the success in the field requires hard work and preparation, but those are the most basic ingredients in a recipe for success. Achieving the baseline qualifications, such as obtaining a JD, is just that: a baseline. You have not "made it" just because you went to law school, despite any trials and triumphs that you encountered to get there and get through it. Law school is much closer to the beginning of the journey than it is to the end. Unfortunately, there are not many resources for those looking for a career serving the public interest as to what the journey looks like or what those next steps on the path are. Your ultimate success as an attorney and advocate will depend on your investment in yourself and execution of your strategy. Using materials that you are already required to develop is a strategic way to gauge your progress. Your reading this book means you are off to a great start.

2

What Is a Public Interest Lawyer?

Public interest law is a catchall term for what is actually an extensive and all-encompassing area of the profession. In its broadest sense, public interest lawyers tend to work on behalf of families and individuals in need, whether it be in relation to criminal matters (through public defender offices) or civil matters (often through civil legal aid organizations). When it comes to advocacy, public interest lawyers tend to advocate on behalf of those historically excluded from traditional halls and tables of power. This is why "public interest" attorney is a bit of a misnomer, as public interest attorneys practice across settings and/or have expertise in all types of substantive areas of law.

The opportunities in public interest are endless, so the most important thing you can do as a law student or young attorney is develop an understanding of the many types of practice settings and identify the type of substantive work you are interested in doing. There are many types of roles that public interest attorneys can fulfill, including different types of litigation and client representation. Direct services refers to client-based representation, where attorneys often perform intake and represent individual clients in court. Direct service work requires strong interpersonal skills and cultural humility to relate to clients, as well as competencies in writing and oral advocacy. Given shifts in national demographics, it is increasingly important for attorneys providing direct representation to have knowledge of a language other than English. Appellate advocacy involves analyzing outcomes at trial and strategizing with clients to narrow the best issues to win on appeal; this often involves drafting briefs and then arguing in front of the appellate court. Class actions or impact litigation, on the other hand, often involve developing legal strategy and selecting a class of plaintiffs to build cases from scratch, conducting investigations, drafting motions and briefs, conducting depositions and settlement negotiations, and arguing before the court. In these cases, the public framing tends to be as important as the case itself, so attorneys on these cases often draft public communications such as blogs, op-eds, or press releases.

Law students and young attorneys may also be interested in a public interest career centered on policy and legislative advocacy. Much of this advocacy is often issue-based or rooted in constitutional rights. In this capacity, attorneys often participate in the policymaking process by conducting research and authoring reports, white papers, testimony, or education materials on substantive or procedural issues. These materials are often used in meetings with government officials across the three branches of government to advise them on issues or to lobby them to take certain action on legislation or regulations. Other aspects of policy or legislative advocacy involve strategizing to bring people to the table to develop consensus about an issue, working within communities to bring their interests and needs to the attention of government officials, and drafting bills, regulations, or other policies to advance a position on an issue. In addition, there are a number of public interest lawyers who work on issues in an enforcement, oversight, or accountability capacity; practice settings for these attorneys may be government agencies, special oversight commissions, offices of inspectors general, or non-governmental organizations, which may require attorneys to employ skills in investigations, audits, document review, and possibly litigation. It is important to note that many policy and legislative positions are considered nonpracticing. This is more of a reflection of traditional, limited notions about what it means to be a "real" attorney and the practice of the law then it is a reflection of what the work requires. You should always address this at the negotiation stage when you receive an offer, as whether your organization considers you a practicing attorney may inform salary, benefits (e.g., student loan forgiveness), and internal professional opportunities.

When people think of practice settings for public interest lawyers, they often think of lawyers who are employed by the government at either the local, state, or federal level. This covers public defenders, prosecutors, and those who work in attorneys general offices or other administrative agencies. Other public interest lawyers work on behalf of poor individuals or families with legal problems, such as people facing eviction, foreclosure, a denial of public benefits, or child custody issues. Many legal aid organizations receive government funding to provide free civil legal assistance to qualified low-and middle-income individuals; many of these organizations are regional or local in nature. Other organizations are funded through either foundations or private donors.

Outside of government, public interest attorneys can also work for nonprofit or non-governmental organizations. Many of these organizations work on behalf of civil rights and social justice issues on a national scale. For example, attorneys at class action or impact litigation shops like the American Civil Liberties Union, the NAACP Legal Defense and Education Fund, the Advancement Project, the Southern Poverty Law Center, and the Lawyer's Committee on Civil Rights often litigate cases with the goal of broader impact or structural change. Likewise, organizations like Earthjustice or the National Resources Defense Council use litigation as a tool to champion environmental justice, while organizations like Protect Democracy and the Campaign Legal Center litigate in furtherance of the public interest by protecting democratic institutions, limiting money in politics, and expanding access to voting. These organizations do not do a lot of direct representation unless it furthers positions with broader implications, instead preferring class actions or appellate advocacy. However, there are a variety of organizations situated regionally or within communities that are uniquely positioned to provide direct representation or otherwise advocate on behalf of clients to provide assistance in areas most relevant to the local community, such as Public Counsel in Los Angeles, the Georgia Justice Project, or the Texas Civil Rights Project, while many others work across issues such as human rights, LGBTQ+ equality, education, housing justice, children's rights, and immigrants' rights.

Regardless of the type of legal advocacy organization, there is a growing trend in the field to move toward engaging in legislative policy and advocacy. This is often an acknowledgement of the limitations of litigation and judicial remedies and a reflection of the complementary role of the legislative branch in social change. While some organizations have their staff attorneys engage in this work, it is becoming increasingly common to hire attorneys as policy counsels, legislative counsels (or similar titles) with specific skills (e.g., political acumen, coalition building, bill drafting, and a command of constitutional law) to advance their agendas. Moreover, there are several nonprofit advocacy organizations and non-governmental organizations that do not represent clients or litigate where attorneys push for legislative and policy on issues concerning human rights and social justice.

There are also a growing number of organizations that are shifting to integrated advocacy models to amplify their impact. In legal advocacy organizations looking for big structural change, this often means employing a combination of impact litigation, policy and legislative advocacy, organizing, and communications work. For direct service providers, integrated advocacy can take the form of direct representation in collaboration with a social work or counseling team that is tasked with meeting all the various needs of a client. This can range from immediate needs such as food, shelter, or medical care or long-term needs such as child support, public benefits, employment, or housing. These organizations tend to attract inter- and multi-disciplinary talent that creatively approaches societal problems through a different lens.

Regardless of the type of public interest setting you intend to practice in, it is important to understand the pathway into the field and develop a plan.

HOW DO I BECOME A PUBLIC INTEREST LAWYER?

In addition to attending law school, the pathway to becoming a public interest attorney involves developing the skills and competencies necessary to fulfill the roles. As you are looking for positions serving the public interest it will be necessary to demonstrate a sense of commitment to an organization's mission or a greater sense of individual purpose that informs your passion to be a public interest attorney. One way that law students demonstrate commitment is through the courses they take. For example, a student looking to become a prosecutor or public defender may take advanced courses in criminal law and criminal procedure, while a student looking to go the impact litigation route may take advanced courses in constitutional law, civil practice, federal courts, and legal writing. Another way to demonstrate commitment to a cause is through extracurricular activities such as participation in student groups, pro bono legal services, or nonlegal volunteer work with community-based organizations. Students also demonstrate their commitment to working in the public interest through their clinical experience or externships. This is not to say that if you do not take these courses or participate in these extracurriculars that you will not be qualified to enter the public interest legal field. However, through strategic course selection and the purposeful pursuit of opportunities, an intentional law student or young attorney can tell a dynamic story.

It is also important to consider where you will begin your career and what you hope to get out of your formative years as a young attorney. While government agencies tend to have tracks for truly entry-level, fresh-out-of-law-school positions, many nonprofit organizations do not. The reality is that many nonprofit advocacy organizations are not actually great training grounds for new attorneys, as limitations in staff, funding, and resources often lead these employers to look for staff that already have relevant experience or can otherwise demonstrate that they can hit the ground running. Because there are so few opportunities for applicants to demonstrate this with any certainty, employers often impute this from other factors such as law school ranking, reputation, GPA, or other marker with a similar connotation of competence. This makes many public interest organizations very insular. While internships are important to gain exposure and practical experience throughout law school, the key to obtaining full-time positions at many nonprofit legal advocacy organizations is often fellowships.

Over the past decade public interest legal fellowships have risen in popularity—and prestige. While some public interest employers, such as larger public defender or prosecutor offices, can hire entry-level attorneys in classes, many employers hire only a handful of positions annually, if at all. Public interest legal fellowships are short-term engagements that allow recent graduates to work at an employer for a term-limited period often capped at two years. During this time, legal fellows gain experience working for an organization in a more in-depth capacity than typical internships or externships allowed for. Fellows are a part of the staff and can gain access to the amenities and benefits that permanent employees enjoy while gaining substantive expertise through in-depth exposure to an area of law. These fellowships can be sponsored by the organization itself, by big law firms, or by outside philanthropic entities; fellowships can also be sponsored post-graduate opportunities connected to law schools.

The day-to-day experiences of fellows may differ depending on an organization's needs and structure. During some fellowships, a young attorney will focus on a particular project that is a priority to the organization but they have not yet had the capacity to undertake. In other fellowships young attorneys may take on cases in a particular practice area or be tasked with exploring a new area of work for the organization. It is important to understand that while fellowships are tailored to recent graduates, many organizations are not great training grounds, as they can sometimes operate using trial by fire. As such, it is important to understand what you need from a supervisor and a potential employer to be successful. Knowing what you need from a supervisor is not an easy task. It begins with reflection and clarity on your goals, a sense of self-awareness, and an ability to self-assess both strengths and weaknesses. The things you need from a supervisor should change as you grow throughout your career as a law student and then enter the legal profession. For example, as a law student interning for the first time in the field, you may want a supervisor who is more hands-on and has the capacity to provide detailed feedback on your writing and analysis. An attorney a few years out of law school may be seeking a supervisor to develop their motion practice or someone who has the time to develop them into a supervisor themselves. Regardless of the need, it is important to try your best to ask these questions at the interview stage and to follow up with ongoing, open, transparent conversation once you are in the position. When done right, these fellowship positions can unlock future opportunities that can truly make your career and set you on a trajectory to accomplish all your professional goals.

A BIT ON SALARY

If you are interested in becoming an attorney to get rich, a path in public interest law may not be for you. Starting salaries and salary ranges can vary. There are resources such as Glassdoor, a company that promotes transparency in pay and workplace environment through anonymous employee reviews, and Payscale, a company that analyzes compensation trends using big data to provide tools for both employers and job seekers, that can provide a starting place for research on a position or industry. For example, Payscale lists the national average salary of an entry-level public interest lawyer with less than one year of experience as $69,143 in 2022.[1] Again, this number can vary widely depending on the specific job an attorney holds. Other considerations for difference in salary include geographic location, such as what state you are working in, and whether you are practicing in an urban, suburban, or rural area; the cost of benefits, such as whether an employer fully covers the costs of health care or how high the retirement match is; management or supervisory responsibilities, whether that is a large or complex caseload or managing people; and whether you are admitted to the bar or need to become licensed, as some employers have graduate pay scales for entry-level employees.

When considering any opportunity, it is important to consider total compensation, not just salary, and to have a clear understanding of your financial situation. Not everything about compensation will be up for negotiation, but it is important to always negotiate and to do so strategically. As an attorney you are expected to have solid negotiation skills and, as the preferred candidate, this is your first attempt to demonstrate to an employer how you would approach a negotiation.

Given the realities of the cost of law school, it is easy to understand why many law students and young attorneys feel like a career in public interest law is out of reach. But remember, entry-level salaries are not forever, and you don't need to repay your student loans in one lump-sum payment. Once you have gained expertise,

[1] https://www.payscale.com/research/US/Job=Lawyer%2C_Public_Interest/Salary.

established yourself as an expert, or taken on supervisory responsibilities, there is often significant room for growth in salary, often into the six-figure range depending on your organization and where you are located. For example, an entry-level attorney at the U.S. Department of Justice who has clerked for at least two years is eligible to be brought in at a Grade 13, Step 1 (GS-13), which meant a starting salary of $81,216 in 2022.[2] This salary then increases as you gain more experience and remain with the government. Nonetheless, the attorneys I have seen who are most satisfied with their careers are those who have followed their passion and interests; for the majority of them, salary has followed.

As understandably important as salary is, I would strongly discourage someone from choosing a career path solely based on money. If you are faced with two great opportunities that are aligned with your career goals, then it makes sense to perhaps place a greater emphasis on salary and benefits. Sometimes, however, we are faced with choices between an opportunity that aligns with our interests and goals but doesn't pay well, and another that perhaps pays well but isn't as aligned with our goals. It is completely understandable that there will be times when you need to choose the money, but the money should not determine every decision. Discernment and a personal commitment to your destination (i.e., career goal, position, impact) will be what is most important. No one can tell you the right choice to make, and there are many different roads to a destination. Always make sure that any opportunity carries you further down a road to your destination in terms of position and impact, and not off the path, no matter how flashy the pitstop.

---

[2] U.S. Dept. of Justice. Entry-level (Honors Program) and Experienced Attorney, *Attorney Salaries, Promotions, and Benefits* (n.d.), *available at* https://www.justice.gov/legal-careers/attorney-salaries-promotions-and-benefits (last updated December 1, 2020).

TIP: GET A FINANCIAL ADVISOR (AND AN ACCOUNTANT).

Once you graduate law school, you are in the "real world." It is important to have a deep understanding of your financial situation before making any financial decisions, and that includes accepting a job or other opportunity with financial implications. Financial advisors are not just for people who are wealthy or high-income earners. A financial advisor can help you develop a game plan to conquer your student loan debt, save for retirement, and prop you up to become financially stable. Understanding your financial situation as you are navigating new opportunities can help give you a leg up in your negotiations. This knowledge can help you decide whether to emphasize your base salary, retirement contributions, or other aspects of your total compensation, and craft your plan accordingly. Remember, you almost always want an employer to increase your base salary, rather than offer a signing bonus. You should also inquire about benefits such as reimbursement for cell phone or internet expenses, repayment assistance for student loans, or child care assistance for work-related travel.

Financial advisors can also be helpful with contingency plans. Rainy day funds have a number of uses: unexpected layoff, medical leave, or family support, to name a few. However, a rainy day fund can also provide you with flexibility and serve the dual purpose of being a "go to hell" fund. It is occasionally the case that an organization may go in a direction you are not interested in or do something that compromises your values. In these instances, your "go to hell" fund can buy you the time to secure your next opportunity without feeling compelled to stay in a place that no longer aligns with your values and mission.

3

Developing a Career Strategy

> "If you don't know where you're going, you'll probably end up somewhere else."
>
> —Yogi Berra

This book is meant to be a one-stop shop for early career development for law students and new attorneys seeking to build a career in nonprofits and public interest law. This chapter will lay out a philosophy on career development and branding by relying on traditional application materials; that is, your résumé and cover letter. This strategic approach to using your résumé and cover letter to guide your career development and success can bolster your professional reputation, also referred to as your brand. Professional branding refers to developing, establishing, and promoting the skills, talents, and contributions you ultimately want to be known for. The beauty of using your résumé and cover letter is that they are already formatted to highlight key aspects of professional development and personal growth. For example, the education section functions to lay the foundation of your relevant experience. In this section law students and young lawyers can begin to demonstrate both their qualifications and their commitment. This is especially true for law students and young attorneys who have a bit more liberty in terms of what they can include. For example, it is common for a law student's education section to include courses taken, extracurricular activities, honors, and GPA/ranking.

It is important that you utilize your Education section early in your career to lay the foundation for your story and stand out in the proverbial crowd. Remember, no one expects you to know anything of consequence as a 1L applying for their first internship, and your ability to stand out as a 1L is limited because people mostly take the same classes. However, as you move through law school you will be able to bolster this section with information that illustrates how you spend your law school experience outside of the classroom. Your education section will necessarily shorten as you move further into your career and items become stale. Details such as extracurricular activities and GPA tend not to be included in the résumés of more seasoned attorneys. Considerations about what to include in your education section are discussed in more detail in chapter 5.

The experience section is where you begin to tell your professional story. This section should be used to illustrate your growth and skill acquisition over time, as well as how/why those skills are important (read: impact and outcomes). For example, in your first position you may be responsible for assisting with responses to the organization's legal intake. As you become more familiar with the process you may grow into tasks of conducting intake meetings and issue spotting. Similarly, you may start one position tasked with legal research to update a know-your-rights presentation, but eventually grow to deliver such trainings on behalf of the organization. As you are capturing this experience for your résumé you should be sure to include details about the subject and audience. For instance, a résumé line may read, "Delivered a series of know-your-rights trainings on police–citizen interactions to high school students attending school in over-policed neighborhoods." You may also have a section for volunteer experience, or service, where you can further link your passions and interests to your professional experiences.

People often say you should stay ready so you don't need to get ready. When someone presents you with an opportunity, the last thing you should need to say is, "Man, I really need to update my résumé." Your résumé is a working document, but you should make sure it is always in a position to be sent out on a whim, should an opportunity present itself. However, because it is a working document it will also always benefit from editing and feedback. A young attorney once reached out to me for professional advice, and during our session I suggested some changes to their résumé. They were a bit put off and responded, "My résumé has landed me every position I've ever had." They were completely closed to feedback. I surmise that statement is true for everyone who has landed a job they actually had to apply for. But unless that résumé has landed an offer from every job you have applied for, or at least an interview from every place you have applied to, there is likely room for feedback and improvement. (And, to be honest, if that particular young attorney was perfectly content with their position, they would not have been reaching out to me in the first place.) It is perfectly normal to be defensive about your experience, but part of career growth and development is the ability to solicit feedback, hear it, move through the discomfort, and devise a strategy to address any issues and improve.

> Discomfort is a natural part of both job searching and professional development. A natural part of the job application process—and your professional development journey—is learning where you are lacking in skills and abilities. Learning these things about yourself may be uncomfortable, and sometimes this feedback may be delivered in a manner that seems harsh or unfair. However, this is necessary to experience. People won't always be nice to you, but you need to learn how to discern feedback that is constructive from that which is intended to tear you down. Not everyone who is nice to you has your best interest at heart. Not everyone who is harsh harbors ill will towards you. Being able to move through this discomfort and not take it personally is an invaluable skill for professional growth and development.

People also say don't dress for where you are, dress for where you're going. A similar thing can be said about résumés: You don't need a résumé to reflect where you are, you need your résumé to showcase where you can go. The vibe of your résumé should strike the balance of showcasing the skills you possess and the accomplishments you have achieved, while also giving a clear sense of what you can do but have not yet done. My approach to career development is rather straightforward. It consists of three parts: 1) start with yourself, 2) be the preferred candidate, and 3) demonstrate growth and personal investment with a 1 + 1 approach.

START WITH YOURSELF

All journeys start with the beginning. In this spirit, the first prong of my strategy is to start with yourself. Starting with yourself means doing some reflection to envision the career you want to have. In order to successfully build a brand, you should have an image of what you are aspiring to. For some people, this may mean literally envisioning your future. For example, when I was in college, I laid out a general vision for my career: to attend a distinguished law school and work for a national nonprofit impacting positive change on the lives of Black people. For others, it may mean listing specifics, such as the impact you want to have on the world or the profession. In other words, what do you want to have happened or want to be true by virtue of you having done a job or held a position? Try to put it in a sentence. As it pertains to this book, my sentence would be: *Because I wrote this book, a generation of law students and young attorneys will have the tools to succeed as public interest attorneys, regardless of where they attended law school or whether they had a mentor or a preexisting strong professional network.* The most important part of this process is to be clear and specific.

Oftentimes young attorneys have strong, though vague, ideas about where they should work, what prestigious fellowship or coveted internship they need to obtain, how much money they should earn, and so on. Many of these ideas are driven by interpretations of what they think success in the legal profession looks like. What many law students fail to do is think deeply about what they want their career to be and why. A career in nonprofits and public interest often requires a sense of commitment and purpose beyond just "wanting to help people." Many nonprofit and public interest attorneys are on the frontlines of our nation's trauma. Whether it is fighting to keep families from being separated at the border, to keep clients out of jail, or to promote policies that can transform and change lives, each day can be challenging. A sense of purpose will not get you through it for the long haul but understanding what you have signed up for as a career, and being intentional in your purpose (i.e., your "why"), can keep you energized and centered.

Professional Branding

As previously mentioned, professional branding means developing, establishing, and promoting the skills, talents, and contributions you ultimately want to be known for. If you are unsure of a place to start, I suggest asking yourself the simple question: *What do I want my professional brand to be?* In other words, what do you want to be known for? When I ask this question of law students and young attorneys I often hear, "to be a good attorney." In these instances I always probe further to ask them to be more specific. The clearer the vision, the easier it is to understand the burgeoning brand. Some people want to brand themselves based on substantive knowledge and issue expertise. Others establish their brands based on a set of skills; for example, trial lawyers. For example, one young man saw a need and established himself as the go-to advocate around expungements and equitable policymaking and regulation in the context of marijuana legalization and licensing. Some attorneys anchor their brands in a particular geographic area, such as being the go-to tenant's rights attorney in a given region. Regardless of the vision, the next step will be ordering your steps to bring your goals to fruition.

BE THE PREFERRED CANDIDATE

The second prong of my strategy is to be the person employers prefer. Being the preferred candidate refers to strategically seeking opportunities that will build the skills needed to match your qualifications to the list of desired competencies above the baseline expectations of your target opportunity. As a law student, seeking opportunities that build the skills of the preferred candidate means taking the right classes, participating in a journal, volunteering, and working in internships that help to introduce you to a particular issue area, practice setting, or skill set. As you move through your career, if there is a gap in your experience that leads you to present as less than qualified for your targeted (or dream) position, you should take interim steps to seek opportunities to equip yourself with that particular skill or set of experiences. For example, if you are seeking a position where appellate advocacy is necessary, you can try to seek pro bono experience representing a client's appeal. As discussed later, you may also identify gaps in your experience through feedback from interviews. Keep your eyes on the prize and use this information to provide clarity on what you need to get out of your next opportunity. This necessarily requires you going for "reach" positions that will stretch your skill set and require you to perform new tasks or old tasks in new ways. Embrace this process.

In the context of seeking opportunities, there are gendered differences in approaches to potential opportunities. When a job comes up, men tend to be more likely to apply for a position, even if they don't meet the requisite qualifications. Women, on the other hand, tend to not apply.[1] During former First Lady Michelle Obama's tour on her memoir *Becoming*, she reflected on her experiences with imposter syndrome and recounts, "I have been at probably every powerful table that you can think of, I have worked at nonprofits, I have been at foundations, I have worked in corporations, served on corporate boards, I have been at G summits, I have sat in at the U.N.: They are not that smart."[2] A part of being the preferred candidate is overcoming impostor syndrome to the best of your ability and recognizing, with confidence, that you belong. While I don't purport to be able to solve gender differences in seeking opportunities, I do strongly believe that a solid career development plan can help prevent imposter syndrome and reassure candidates, especially women and underrepresented minorities, that they meet the qualifications.

---

[1] Tara Sophia Mohr, *Why Women Don't Apply to Jobs Unless They're 100% Qualified*, HARVARD BUSINESS REVIEW (Aug. 25, 2014), https://hbr.org/2014/08/why-women-dont-apply-for-jobs-unless-theyre-100-qualified.

[2] https://www.newsweek.com/michelle-obama-tells-secret-i-have-been-every-powerful-table-you-can-think-1242695.

The way to do this is to know long in advance what the requisite qualifications are for the position you ultimately want to hold. As you are taking steps to advance your career you should simultaneously become confident in your abilities and, thus, go out for opportunities without selling yourself short.

After you envision the career you want to have, you should then identify specific positions or types of positions that embody that ideal future career. For example, if you envision yourself as the director of a legal services organization, then you should locate a couple of job descriptions for such a position in the practice area and at the scale you imagine. For example, if you want to lead a large organization or team, you may look at positions responsible for a certain amount of staff or with an operating budget of over $1 million. Once you have located these job descriptions, examine both the qualifications and the "preferred" qualifications on the résumé and assess which ones you possess and which ones you don't. A critical part of this assessment is not only whether you have done a particular thing, but how well you have done it, whether you have mastered it, and if you can execute it autonomously. The skills or experiences you don't currently have become the target skills to acquire over the next few years to prepare you for the next stage of your career. For example, figure 3.1 is an excerpt of a position description for a legal director of a civil rights and racial justice program at a state legal aid office. You will notice the required qualifications section lists a compendium of baseline experience, such as being admitted to a state bar for five years, familiarity with the criminal legal system, and a "strong commitment to social, economic, and racial justice." For the most part, the qualifications listed as required represent the bare minimum, and most applicants should be able to frame their experience in ways that qualify. The preferred qualifications section, however, includes more specifics in terms of what the organization is expecting of the candidate. These qualifications include experience litigating civil rights issues in federal court, at least three years of experience as a supervisor, and state-level policy advocacy experience, preferably through a race equity lens and involving data. These are the areas of focus in terms of skill-building and development.

FIGURE 3.1 REQUIRED QUALIFICATIONS

While no one candidate will possess all the requirements listed, the ideal candidate will have many of the following qualifications:

- Minimum five years' membership in any state bar; if not admitted in Virginia, must be eligible to waive in or to sit for the Virginia Bar. *(Note, the Virginia Supreme Court will be considering a rule change that would make it easier for legal aid employees licensed in other states to waive into the Virginia Bar.)*
- Mission-aligned experience (work or lived) partnering with and advocating in low-wealth communities and communities of color
- Sincere and demonstrated commitment to racial equity, inclusion, and justice
- Familiarity with criminal legal policy/system (from work or lived experience)
- Ability to work and communicate effectively across lines of identity and difference
- Ability to effectively supervise across lines of identity and difference
- Ability to work effectively both independently and collaboratively
- Strong oral advocacy, research, and writing skills
- Willingness to work a flexible schedule that may include evening and weekend events, as well as occasional travel
- Strong commitment to social, economic, and racial justice

PREFERRED QUALIFICATIONS

- Federal civil rights litigation experience
- Policy advocacy at the agency and legislative level
- Familiarity with organizing campaigns and/or community or movement lawyering
- Prior advocacy experience (work or lived) using an explicit race equity lens
- Minimum three years' prior supervisory experience (in official capacity as supervisor or substantially similar work without official title)
- Comfort with technology and data review

Once you have identified the competencies or experiences you need to have, your next search for a job or other opportunity should be oriented toward finding present opportunities that build up to that experience. But professional development is not just about your 9-to-5. Requisite skills can also be acquired through board service or other volunteer positions with leadership responsibilities. No matter the forum, it is important to make sure that any opportunity will actually prepare you for your future steps and, if it doesn't, to reorient yourself toward other opportunities. For example, if an ideal position requires, on average, ten years' experience supervising attorneys, then you want to seek out a position where it is possible to become a supervisor, even if you only supervise one other attorney.

I hate to see a seasoned attorney looking to launch the next stage of their career but struggling because they just found out they have been working but not growing for the past few years. Seek out present opportunities that provide you with the desired experience for your ideal career to prevent an unfortunate situation. The last thing you want is to arrive at the stage when you are looking to level up into your next professional endeavor and realize you have spent years acquiring experience that is either irrelevant or does not add value to your candidacy. It is one thing to tell a future employer what you can do, but it is always better to *show* them what you can do by providing evidence of tangible skills developed by carrying out similar tasks. Whereas the ability to strategize and carry a project from beginning to end is a requirement, your ability to intentionally develop your career and chart your course for success is certainly evidence of that.

> I want to acknowledge that what I am saying here runs counter to a bevy of advice you have likely received. But, plainly, not all experience is good experience. Sure, there is almost an angle to be played to emphasize the transferrable skills gained. However, why limit yourself to that when, with some planning and intention, you can actually develop the skills being asked for? The answer is, you shouldn't . . . at least not if you can help it.

You often hear people talk about experience, but experience is elusive as a term and, in fact, takes on a number of meanings pertaining to career growth. In one narrow sense of the word, people talk about experience as a proxy for expertise that is most often measured by the number of years as a lawyer. For example, I have often seen job postings looking for experienced attorneys where that translates to being at least seven or more years out of law school. I have also seen employers who are looking for experienced attorneys, but instead are specifically counting experience as the number of years working in a particular position, practicing in a particular practice area, or completing a specific type of task. Impact litigation shops often look for attorneys who have experience filing certain types of complex civil litigation, while some immigration advocacy shops may gauge experience by "U" and "T" visa filings. Having the right type of experience, or being able to signal and make the connections for an employer as to why you are qualified despite the absence of that experience, is a key ingredient to the recipe of success.

Note: This reference to "working but not growing" should not be taken to mean that you need to constantly grow and develop in every position. There are moments in your career (or life) where having a job where you can chill or coast can be beneficial for a number of reasons. Perhaps you want to prioritize your family or are deciding whether to go back to school or take up a new hobby that may take time (like writing a book!). It is perfectly fine to build coasting into your professional plan. What I am more so referring to is when people don't intentionally plan their careers, and by the time they realize they are not on course for what they are trying to do, they have lost a lot of time (and eligibility for certain opportunities) because they have been unintentionally coasting for years.

Being the preferred candidate, however, is about more than just having the right experience. In addition to possessing technical skills, an organization's preferred candidate also embodies a clear commitment to their mission. Earlier I discussed that law students or young attorneys looking to enter a public interest career can demonstrate their commitment to mission through experience, extracurricular activities, and/or service to the profession or the community. But it is important to note that there are wrong ways to demonstrate this commitment. For example, some law students try to boost their résumés by participating in as many activities they can. Keep in mind, public interest organizations can often see right through résumé boosting, or accumulating experiences and accreditations just to check a box and attempt to bolster their résumé. This is especially so if you make it to the interview stage. Résumé boosting can often backfire by giving the impression that you are either scattered or not committed to a particular cause or activity. In the conversation that is an interview, it is easy to tell which candidates are just boosting their résumés and which have substance. It is better to participate in an activity and stick with it as best you can than to jump around or only participate on paper. As will be discussed later, you should make sure that you are able to speak intelligently and in detail to each item listed on your résumé.

TIP: BECAUSE YOUR RÉSUMÉ WILL BE TWO PAGES AT MOST, PRIOR WINS MAY FALL OFF AS TIME GOES ON AND YOU ACHIEVE NEW HEIGHTS IN YOUR CAREER. This is natural. As I discuss in chapter 6, every word counts. You don't need to capture everything you've ever done at a job, only the responsibilities or achievements most relevant to demonstrating that you are the preferred candidate for your next position.

Hiring managers are often tasked with identifying candidates aligned with the mission, so the preferred candidate not only has the credentials, they can also communicate an understanding of the organization and how it actually does its work. For example, an organization that utilizes a community lawyering model may be interested in a candidate with a background in organizing or community outreach and engagement. However, it is not enough to possess the experience, the candidate should be able to communicate how those experiences have prepared them to engage in community lawyering and how doing so fulfills the organization's mission. The ability to speak to how your background aligns with an organization's needs can signal to an employer that you are the preferred candidate.

Regardless of how a potential opportunity is defining experience, you want to make sure you are prepared. The best way to do this is to make sure you are leveling up your skill and experience each year. Demonstrating growth over time is a great way to remain competitive over the course of your career.

DEMONSTRATE GROWTH WITH A 1 + 1 APPROACH

It is important to strive to be the preferred candidate for each opportunity and at each stage in your career. To make sure you are growing on pace to achieve your career goals, law students and young attorneys should adopt what I call a 1 + 1 approach. The 1 + 1 approach refers to the ability to measure career growth using the experience and service sections of your résumé. As a rule of thumb, you should master a skill, acquire a new one, take on additional responsibilities, or have a demonstrable or quantifiable win to add to your experience section each year. Similarly, you should maintain or add one service opportunity per year, either to the profession or to the community. Ideally, your service opportunity should demonstrate escalating responsibility, leadership, and impact. Doing this is important to keep you competitive, but more importantly, this approach will help prevent stagnation in your positions. People often wonder how they know when it is time to transition. A tell-tale sign that it is time to move on from a position is when you are no longer learning new things, taking on new challenges, and racking up new wins.

Using a 1 + 1 approach can help you hold yourself accountable to goals you've set for your own personal growth and professional development. Tracking your growth over time allows you to see where you started and continue to work toward getting to where you are trying to go. One way to do this is the keep a master résumé, where you hold the universe of information you may want to include. This should not just be a static list of positions. Instead, it should be dynamic and capture detailed descriptions of your experience in every section. For example, the education section should house your list of relevant courses, student activities, clinics, awards, or publications. Use the experience section to list every position you've ever held. Do not impose traditional limitations on the length of a description of job duties; instead include every relevant duty and outcome. The details are important because they will become the basis by which you will track your growth to becoming the preferred candidate. And each new experience should clearly build upon previous experience to demonstrate steady skill acquisition and mastery over time.

You may be wondering how to know what skills you need to develop in order to become the preferred candidate. As demonstrated by the previous example, the answer is simpler than you think. The majority of job postings actually include desired qualifications. Use this information to your advantage. Employers tell you what they are looking for and you can use these job postings to identify skills to build your long-term growth strategy. It is likely the case that as you move up the ladder or advance in your career an employer will be seeking skills outside of those that are strictly legal. Skill building necessarily includes both hard and soft skills. At the start of your career it is most prudent to focus on developing hard skills. By the time you are a mid-level attorney (approximately five to seven years out of law school), employers will assume you know how to write a brief, conduct legal research, or do anything else fundamental to your practice. As you are advancing in your career, soft skills begin to increase in significance, especially if you are looking to transition into more autonomous roles or leadership positions. For example, if you are seeking to lead a team, intercultural fluency is likely expected. Other soft skills that may be important are problem solving, public speaking, mentorship, or exceptional relationship skills. Remember, as you are ascending in your career people will be looking for qualities and experiences that demonstrate you can lead, develop, and grow other people. Such skills may include the supervision of other supervisors, grant writing for operational support of programs, or the management of program budgets. Remember, a good leader can do more than just keep the ship running.

TIP: KEEPING A MASTER RÉSUMÉ CAN ALSO HELP YOU IN SALARY NEGOTIATIONS WITH A POTENTIAL EMPLOYER LATER DOWN THE LINE.

Many employers have salary bands or "step" compensation where you are placed in the range based on a combination of education and experience. A master résumé enables you to approach negotiations more strategically by having tangible examples of your experience and qualifications, which will substantiate your ask. See chapter 6 for more information.

In crafting your long-term strategy you should consider opportunities to obtain this broader experience through both professional and volunteer endeavors. Do not be afraid to side-hustle your skills! One young attorney seeking to transition into a supervisory position decided to gain leadership skills and experience managing a budget by joining the finance committee of the board they served on. When it came time to interview for the position, they were able to detail their experience overseeing budgets in a fiduciary capacity. Another young transactional attorney for a national corporate law firm began volunteering with a medical legal clinic on the weekends to prepare for a transition into health-care policy. Every position that you take on should move you further along toward your goals, but it requires intention.

> **Note:** The advice that each position move you along toward your goal is not résumé boosting. On the contrary, this is more about moving with intention and amplifying your impact throughout your career. As you gain more skills and experience you should be able to better leverage them for impact.

The Relationship between Résumés and Career Development

Résumés are more of a tool for career development than people realize. Not only do they document your experience, they also chronicle your career trajectory. An understanding of this relationship signals certain traits to an employer—especially those that are mission-driven—about a candidate's values, commitment, and intentionality. Your résumé can showcase growth in a number of areas of interest to an employer, such as a growth in lawyering skills, substantive expertise, managerial or supervisory responsibilities, or tangible impact. Growth demonstrated by lawyering skills refers to increased proficiency at fundamental (and universal) skills such as legal research and writing and oral advocacy. Demonstrating growth as measured by substantive expertise refers to increasing knowledge of a particular area of law, the legal field or public interest landscape, or the business of the organization where you are employed. Candidates often showcase growth in their supervisory capabilities by having shifted from onboarding interns to supervising attorneys and support staff to supervising other supervisors. Similarly, managerial skill growth can be demonstrated by managing budgets and programs of increasing size and capacity. Being able to showcase growth through tangible impact requires tracking quantifiable metrics such as clients served, money won, laws passed, or similar relevant outcomes. It is for this reason that using your application materials to employ my strategy can be so effective.

4

Your Résumé Is a Physical Manifestation of Your Brand

A common misconception of résumés is thinking they are merely a summary of your experience. And while résumés do summarize experience, they can do so much more than that. By applying the strategy outlined in this book, you will be able to use your résumé (and cover letter) to guide your professional development, launch your career, and track your growth over time. Whether you are a new attorney entering the job market, or an attorney with a bit of experience looking to leverage it toward that next step, your résumé is a physical manifestation of your brand. As your own brand manager, you want to be cognizant of your reputation and the way others experience you. You also want to be intentional about how you grow your brand in terms of both recognition and reputation. While writing your résumé you should always consider your audience and ask yourself what you want a reader to understand about you.

Your résumé will, of course, demonstrate your experience to date. But it should also give a reviewer a clear sense of what you are capable of. In other words, your résumé serves the dual purpose of showcasing where you've been, while being a roadmap for where you are going, how you are going to get there, and what an employer can expect of you when you arrive. Being a successful attorney only partly depends on your substantive knowledge. And, truthfully, with more attorneys fresh out of law school after coming straight from college, fewer have substantive expertise of any kind. At this stage in your career, it is even more critical to begin to deliberately build a brand; one aspect of your brand should be substantive knowledge. This substantive knowledge will be developed through your work experience (i.e., your day job), though it can be augmented with other experience.

By far, the easiest way to build your reputation in this industry is to do good work. As such, it is critical that you make sure you are meeting—if not exceeding—performance objectives set by your employer. Once you are doing this, one strategy to build your brand is to seek out opportunities to share that knowledge. This can mean authoring an article, participating in a panel, recording a podcast, organizing a conference, or delivering a know-your-rights presentation. The key is to put yourself out there on your issue area. Other ways to share that knowledge include mentoring, pro bono service, or serving on a nonprofit board. Doing good work and strategically making yourself known will continue to open doors for you to build your brand, potentially amplifying your impact.

THE FIRST IMPRESSION (ON PAPER)

Your résumé is the first impression you make on a potential reviewer of your materials. Whether that impression is on a future employer, a reviewer for a fellowship opportunity, an awards committee, or a board president for a service opportunity, your résumé is often the first touch point for a potential opportunity. It may be hard to believe at the outset, but the legal profession is small. (If you are an attorney of color the profession is even smaller, and if you are a woman of color the profession is even smaller than that.) Putting your best foot forward includes an on-brand résumé and cover letter. I've participated in many hiring processes where the difference between making it past the screening phase or to the next round of interviews is how well put together an applicant's materials are.

It is a common misconception that the interview is the time to make a first impression on an employer. In reality, unless an employer is working with a recruiter, your application materials are the first point of contact and, thus, constitute a first impression. To be sure, people aren't often offered an interview if their application does not pass muster. An applicant's materials may not pass muster for a variety of reasons, many outside of an applicant's control. These reasons could range from unconventional résumé formats, typos, and grammatical errors, to schools attended or previous positions held. There is no way to account for everything that may knock you out of the running. Instead, your task as a candidate is to put forth your best application to minimize being eliminated for reasons entirely within your control. While you cannot change your credentials, such as where you obtained your undergraduate degree, you can control misspelling a company name, putting the wrong company name or targeted position title, or lazily forgetting to update a hiring manager's information. Reviewing your materials before submission or, even better, having a friend or colleague review them, is a great strategy to keep you in the race. While many find applying for a job or other opportunity to be daunting, I encourage you to look at it as yet another opportunity to leave a great impression, build your brand, and expand your network.

WILL AN EMPLOYER ELIMINATE YOU OVER A TYPO?

In short, yes. It is not always the case, and it can be dependent on a reviewer, but yes, some employers will end your candidacy over a typo. However, it is important that candidates understand that such actions are often less about typos themselves and more so about the message that the typo's existence sends to an employer. For example, an employer looking for a mid-level or senior attorney who can review other attorney work product for approval can infer that a candidate whose materials have a typo may not be ready for such responsibility. Other messages that a typo can send to a reviewer can include a candidate not taking pride in their work or not caring or being serious enough to review their materials.

A solid résumé and overall application can elevate your candidacy from obscurity into the potential interview pool. But the reverse is also true, and a mediocre résumé—even one that reflects "good" experience—can eliminate you from consideration in the résumé review phase. Shoddy presentation of your materials can also put colleagues or internal advocates in precarious positions, even if they would otherwise vouch for your candidacy and know that you would excel in the position. When people sit on hiring committees they are in positions of power, but how much power they have often depends on internal office dynamics and their track record. For example, an attorney in a supervisory or executive leadership position often has more juice than the fifth-year attorney who is serving on the hiring panel for the first time. If that fifth-year, new-to-the-committee attorney is your "inside man," but you have submitted a poorly written résumé and a recycled cover letter, it will be hard for them to go to bat for you without potentially losing credibility. Even someone with a track record of great hires must use their power to advocate sparingly so they maintain their power on the committee. It isn't personal, but instead a function of office politics and an almost universal dynamic of hiring committees. In short, submitting top-notch materials cannot only increase your chances of a callback, but also make it easier for mentors and sponsors with a seat at the table to open the door for you. While they don't know you personally, your materials are the first impression you will make on their colleagues, so it is imperative you put your best foot forward on all fronts, starting with a résumé that represents a solid brand.

WHAT IS "GOOD" EXPERIENCE?

Despite the potential to reinforce elitism and hierarchy in the public interest legal arena, some employers still place emphasis on certain aspects of candidate experiences that signify the quality of a candidate. In other words, there are certain experiences, such as earning a Skadden Fellowship, attending an Ivy League undergraduate school, or graduating from a T-14 law school, that give an implicit stamp of approval on a résumé. These qualifications tend to be universally recognized as "good" experience.

KNOW YOUR AUDIENCE

The best way to make a good impression is to know your audience. Getting to know your audience is one of the most important steps in a job search. How well you know and target your audience can often make or break an application. Job applicants will often know their general audience: a hiring manager, potential supervisor, or search committee. However, many applicants spend little time getting to know a bit about their audience past the surface. This not only means knowing who is making the decision, but also knowing the organization or team you are applying for. To do this, you should leverage your network to see who you are in relationship with either at the organization you are targeting or with contacts at the organization. This means scanning both your direct contacts and people who you are personally in a relationship with, but it can also involve utilizing career services offices at your degree-granting institutions, or reaching out through your alumni network. If you do not have a network connection, don't worry; try conducting a LinkedIn search of the company, hiring manager, department or position manager (if different), and members of the potential team. If you can identify someone you may have overlooked who you have more than a casual relationship with, reach out to them to have a candid conversation. During this conversation you should inquire about their experience with the company, express your interest in the available opportunity, and ask for feedback or advice on your application. If you feel that it is appropriate, you may also ask to be connected to someone on the team or in the department hiring for the opportunity. If your brand and reputation are solid, it is often the case that people will volunteer to flag your application for the hiring manager. If the connection you identify is more of a loose associate or acquaintance, you should still reach out and ask for an informational interview to learn more about them and their work.

Note: When job searching you should consider investing in LinkedIn Premium, or at least using the free trial during the critical application phase. This will allow you to do background research anonymously, which may make some job seekers more comfortable. It will also allow you to see who is looking you up. If you see a hiring manager or multiple staff members from the same organization looking you up, that can be an indicator that you are under consideration for a position.

The other way that you demonstrate that you know your audience and are sincerely interested in the opportunity is by submitting an application package that is tailored to the specific organization and position. Reusing résumés and cover letters is more common than people care to admit. It can be tempting to send the same résumé. After all, preparing materials is time consuming and your experience isn't changing, right? WRONG. While your experience section or other information may stay the same, you should make edits to your résumé to reflect keywords or relevant terms from the job posting or company website of the place that you are applying to. This is the bare minimum you should do for each application. It is a relatively low lift with a lot of bang for your buck. On an ongoing basis, you should also update the way you describe your current position. A good time to do this is after a mid-year or annual performance review. Your performance review should highlight your topline achievements of the past year, as well as outline your goals for the upcoming one. The description of your position on your résumé should mirror these topline goals and include quantifiable metrics of success whenever possible. Your goals for the upcoming year should reflect the necessary activities to acquire or strengthen the skills necessary to become the preferred candidate for your future position. Again, use the materials you have to your advantage in order to craft an inimitable application tailored to the opportunity.

Under no circumstances should you ever reuse the entirety of a résumé or cover letter. Even if you are applying for similar positions, or if you are submitting your materials to apply for an award or a position on an organization's board, there is always something you can do to more closely align your experience with the opportunity. As you are in the workforce longer, you should be simultaneously gaining more substantive expertise and racking up more accomplishments. Embrace the 1 + 1 approach: What you have accomplished should be evolving over time, and that growth should be reflected on your résumé. As discussed later in this book, tailoring your résumé could be the difference between "beating the bot" and getting a callback, or having your materials discarded. There is no one-size-fits-all solution to every situation, and your résumé is no different. If you are not tailoring your résumé to the opportunity, you are not putting your best foot forward.

5

The Résumé: The Story of You

This chapter covers the mechanics of résumé writing for law students and young attorneys targeting nonprofit and public interest legal positions. It includes advice on sections to include on your résumé, how to order them, key information to convey, and a discussion of pros and cons to certain styles and formats. Résumé writing is an art and there are certainly conventions that are specific to each field. This book is specifically tailored to the public interest subfield in the legal arena, and this chapter is no different. It contains the fundamentals of what a résumé should contain and general conventions of the field. However, I will also discuss ways to utilize the résumé to convey a personal story that makes your alignment with a target organization's mission and values clear. Even after employing these recommendations, it is always suggested that you have someone in your practice area who is preferably currently or formerly employed by, or otherwise familiar with, your target employer review your materials to ensure their quality.

CRAFTING YOUR STORY

Résumé writing can be daunting, but it doesn't have to be. Assuming that you have some version of a résumé already, you can use that as a basis and then employ these tactics to fine-tune it. Doing so will allow you to stand out for future opportunities. One career hack to make updating your résumé easier is to keep a master résumé of all your experience. The master résumé serves as a compendium of your experience and can be the basis for the résumé you submit to each opportunity you are applying for. In this document you should keep a running list of all the positions you have held, awards you have won, organizations you have volunteered for, and any other information relevant to your professional experience. In this version, do not limit yourself by length. Make sure to include specifics about any metric relevant to measuring success in your subfield, such as how many cases you resolved, people you've supervised, budgets you've managed, bills you've helped pass, or publications you've authored. Gathering this information on an ongoing basis will prepare you to quickly tailor your résumé to an opportunity.

TIP: KEEP A MASTER RÉSUMÉ. DOING SO WILL ALLOW YOU TO QUICKLY:

1. access this information for future versions of your résumé should it become relevant for the position;
2. quantify and summarize your experience; and
3. substantiate your asks during employment negotiations.

Your résumé is intended to be a self-contained document that summarizes your experience, details your wins, and puts your best foot forward to a potential employer. Remember, your résumé is a physical manifestation of your brand. You should kick off your résumé with a bold, well-formatted heading that includes your name, credentials, and contact information. Your résumé will then continue with sections on education and experience. The remaining sections on your résumé will depend on your circumstances. Other sections you may include are those on skills, volunteer or extracurricular experiences, licenses and certifications, publications, or (in rare occasions) references.

The Education Section

The section on education should let an employer know you have the requisite credentials for the opportunity. At a bare minimum you should list the school you attended and the degree you obtained. Law students and young attorneys often include the year each degree was conferred, and there are strategic reasons as to why you may do this early in your career. It is likely that this section will be bulkier while you are a law student or early in your career. Within two post-grad opportunities, or approximately five years, this section will include things like extracurricular activities, Dean's List mentions, and your GPA. However, this section should thin out considerably as you advance in your career and transition into less junior positions. It is also sometimes the case that more seasoned attorneys will drop dates from their education sections.

To illustrate how law students and young attorneys may format this section it is instructive to view examples of education sections from three different résumés. The first example is from a law graduate who was fresh out of law school applying for a first position as a tax attorney. In addition to including the school, location, degree earned, and year of graduation, this person included their GPA and class rank. These items are common for law students and young attorneys to include, and it is beneficial to do so when your GPA and rank are competitive; some reviewers for competitive fellowships, clerkships, or entry-level positions use these items to filter candidates and decide who to interview. However, if it is not required then

Figure 5.1 Sample Education Sections

EDUCATION **SOUTHERN UNIVERSITY LAW CENTER** Baton Rouge, Louisiana

J.D. Candidate, January 2020

GPA: 3.23/4.0 Rank: 12/37

Activities: Southern Law Youth Network Senior Program Strategist

Honors: Dean's List Honors Recipient for Multiple Semesters

Relevant Coursework: Federal Income Tax

LOUISIANA STATE UNIVERSITY Baton Rouge, Louisiana

B.A. in Political Science and African American Studies, December 2012
Activities: College of Humanities and Social Sciences Student Advisory Committee Member

---

EDUCATION

Vermont Law School, South Royalton, VT
Juris Doctor expected, May 2018
Honors & Activities: Member, Black Law Student Assoc., recognized w/ community service award for contributions to broader community; Volunteer, Volunteer Income Tax Association (V.I.T.A.), C.L.E.O. Scholar: Continuing Legal Education Opportunity, Expungement Day Volunteer: Helped with intake at campus-based events to educate Vermonters about how to remove old misdemeanor Possession of Marijuana offenses from their records

DePaul University, Chicago, IL
Bachelor of Arts in Political Science, June 2011
Honors & Activities: Student Association, Member, DePaul Democrats, Moot Court, student government, and debate

---

EDUCATION

Benjamin N. Cardozo School of Law, J.D., June 2014

Concentrations in Constitutional Law and Rights and Criminal Law

University of Arizona, B.A., May 2011

Concentrations in Anthropology, Latin American Studies, and Social Justice Advocacy

I suggest removing them. Both GPA and class ranking are items that can either quickly leave a great impression on a reviewer or have your résumé discarded from the pile. Unless they are unequivocally strong or required by an employer there is little reason to risk it. This person also included activities, honors, and relevant coursework, all of which is common for law students and recent graduates. When included, these items should be clear and concise. Remember, nothing on your résumé should require a reviewer to conduct an internet search.

The second example demonstrates the need for clear descriptions of your experience. This example belongs to a recent graduate, approximately two years out of law school, applying to become a public defender. This person has an extensive honors and activities section but it is too verbose to have impact. First, honors and activities should be separated into separate subsections. Moreover, while you participate in some experiences while you are a law student, it is not necessarily the case that it should go in your education section. For example, the description of participating in Expungement Day is likely better suited for the experience section where there is an opportunity to describe the role that was played, or a "volunteer" or "service" section. The subsection on honors and activities is also inconsistently formatted and includes abbreviations that a reviewer may or may not know. Moreover, the clutter in this section obscures the impact of the contents. This should be avoided at all costs.

The third example is from the résumé of a young attorney approximately six years out of law school, applying to criminal justice policy positions at national legal advocacy organizations as a second post-graduation position. Having had experience in the field, they kept their education section simple, with only the bare minimum required information. Limiting your education section to only include your school, degree, and major is appropriate for this level of experience. It also has the added benefit of freeing up valuable real estate for the rest of the résumé, which will become necessary to convey your accomplishments and demonstrate growth as you advance in your career and change positions down the line.

The Experience Section

The section on experience is to let a reviewer know you are the preferred candidate. Start with the master résumé and then work backwards, by deleting any information that is stale or otherwise not relevant to the position you are applying for. For example, if those high school or college internships don't add value to your current application, delete them. When deleting stale or irrelevant information you should only keep descriptions of your experience that are most relevant to the current job description. As you are writing, make sure it is tailored to reflect keywords and desired competencies.

While there is sometimes variation in how these sections are formatted, there are some conventions. For one, the experience section should be in reverse chronological order, meaning start with your most recent experience first and then work backwards to your earliest experience. You should also list the name of the employer and the dates (month and year) that you worked there. Historically, people have also included the location of their employment; however, as people have become more transient and as remote work has become more common, people are beginning to omit that information. But there are certain situations where it may be strategic to include it. For example, if you are seeking an opportunity in a specific geographic area and you have prior work experience in that geographic area, it may be advantageous to include the location of that experience. Similarly, living or being from an area can also qualify you for positions focused on geographic areas or locales.

When determining what to include in this section, it depends on how your résumé is structured. Some law students and young attorneys opt to have a legal experience section where they include relevant positions since starting law school, and a work experience or other experience section where they include paid work and nonlegal employment. As your task is to use your résumé (and cover letter) to craft a compelling narrative as to why you are the preferred candidate, it often makes sense to have a general experience section that includes all your work experience, paid or unpaid, legal or not. When describing your experience you should include only the standout tasks and accomplishments. Figure 5.2 is a quintessential example of a description with both poorly framed experience and extraneous information. This person spent six lines of valuable space on a resume providing a generic statement that provides no insight into their actual experience. Instead of saying they supported the attorneys or set court dates, this person should have kept it short and framed their experience around significant tasks and impact. Knowing your audience can help you determine how to convey your experience. If you know your audience, you can craft your experience to hone the leadership skills, analytical abilities, public speaking capabilities, or other skills a reviewer is hoping to see.

Figure 5.2 Experience Section

19TH JUDICIAL DISTRICT COURT, Baton Rouge, LA

Docket Clerk/ File Clerk MONTH XXXX – MONTH XXXX

Sent court notices to appear, subpoenas, notices to attorneys, and notices to surety. Set court dates that appeared on daily court dockets. Assisted the public through phone calls, and in-office visits. Supported Assistant Public Defenders, and Assistant District Attorneys. Researched pending and adjudicated court matters.

WHAT DO I DO IF I DON'T HAVE LEGAL EXPERIENCE?

A common question that law students and young attorneys ask is what to do if they don't have legal experience. Do NOT add superfluous or unsolicited information to your résumé to compensate for a lack of experience. The best strategy is to be transparent and forthcoming. Adding nontraditional sections to a résumé (e.g., continuous legal education [CLEs] that you have participated in) can backfire. Though there are small nuances, legal résumés by and large have standard sections and information. Including unsolicited information can potentially give a reviewer the impression you are not only inexperienced, but unfamiliar with the conventions of the field. Instead, try to identify key transferable skills that you have developed through other experience and highlight them throughout your résumé. Once you have prominently displayed your relevant experience on your résumé, you can then use your cover letter to craft your narrative about how your past experience has made you the perfect fit for the current position, despite your nontraditional (or lack of) experience.

Other Sections

In addition to sections on education and experience, law students and young attorneys sometimes include sections on interests, service, skills, languages, or publications. There are many things that work for non-attorney résumés that simply don't work for attorney résumés. This includes the inclusion of summaries or objectives at the top of the résumé, skills sections, and sections on hobbies; the interests section also falls into this bucket. In general, an interests section is unnecessary; it doesn't add much value as to why you are the ideal candidate and can be a silent trigger for a reviewer's implicit bias. Whether to include the other sections depends on your background and trajectory. For example, you may have a section on publications if you served on law review or a journal, or you may have a languages section if you have advanced proficiency or are fluent in a language other than English. In the public interest field, it is common to have a service or volunteer section that lists your pro bono experience, board service, and bar association participation and leadership. Regardless of how you decide to structure your résumé, always remember that if you include something you should be prepared to be asked about it in the interview. I cannot state this strongly enough: Do NOT include information that you cannot speak to at length. The risk of looking like you lied about your experience negates the reward of getting the interview. And remember, knowing your audience will guide your inclusion of only the information most relevant to the position and of interest to a reviewer.

REMEMBER, YOUR RÉSUMÉ IS A LIVING DOCUMENT

You should update the descriptions of each of your listed experiences every time you apply to a different position. The essence of your description should remain the same, but it may suit you to highlight some aspects of the job by rearranging the order in which they appear. This can be a particularly useful strategy for those looking to transition into areas they have perhaps been exposed to in other positions but where that exposure was not a core part of their job responsibilities. For example, if you have primarily practiced tenants' rights but were exposed to work on social security appeals, which you would be doing in the next job, you should rearrange your description to highlight that exposure, as informed by the job announcement. You may also want to substitute some of the language to use buzz words from the job description or website of the place where you are applying. Lastly, remember to keep a running résumé of all your relevant experience, awards, certifications, and so on, so that as opportunities occur you have a reference of all your material at the ready.

TIP: USE THE JOB ANNOUNCEMENT TO INFORM THE ORDER IN WHICH YOU DESCRIBE YOUR EXPERIENCE.

Being the preferred candidate requires that you communicate to a reviewer that you possess the preferred qualifications, which are oftentimes listed in the job announcement. If an employer lists qualifications in a particular order, you should try to mimic that order when describing your experience. Remember, your experience section will be in reverse chronological order, but you can organize your paragraph (or bulleted) description to emphasize the things most important to that employer.

6

The Mechanics of Résumé Crafting

The previous chapter walked through all the component sections on a résumé; this chapter provides global considerations on presentation to best tell your story. Above all, the format should be uniform and consistent. The background should be plain and the headings should be simple. There is no one way to craft and format a résumé, and there are many considerations and decisions to be made. The specific format you choose will be dependent upon individual circumstances. However, there are wrong ways to structure your résumé. Not all formats are conducive to an impressive final product that exemplifies your brand and convinces a reviewer that you are the preferred candidate. What follows is some general advice to guide you through the résumé drafting process.

AVOIDING COMMON RÉSUMÉ PITFALLS

These pitfalls can include:

- Using the same verb repeatedly to describe your experience, or using passive verbs instead of action verbs
- Using "inside baseball" jargon, or obscure technical terms not widely known
- Including information that would require a reviewer to use Google to understand what it is
- Listing every job responsibility in the description of your experience
- Having irregular fonts and formatting, or inconsistent formatting
- Having typos and grammatical errors

EVERY WORD COUNTS

It is important to be as concise as possible throughout your entire résumé, but it is most critical when describing your experience. Each description of your position should adequately reflect your skills and accomplishments. The goal is not to list every little thing you had to do on the job. To the contrary, the goal is to succinctly capture the essence of your past positions and do so in a way that is clear and easy for a potential reviewer to understand. Above all, your story needs to be kept short and sweet. The easiest translation of this advice pertains to page length. This will be discussed more later, but as a rule of thumb, **if you have under ten years of experience you should keep your résumé to one page**. The exception to this is if your experience is truly unique or objectively impressive. Once you possess roughly a decade of experience it can be appropriate for your résumé to extend to two pages. However, you should still be intentional about the use of space, the inclusion of certain sections, and words that you use. A two-page résumé should be just as impactful as a one-page résumé, and your most relevant experience and biggest accomplishments should still stand out to a reviewer skimming through. Most importantly, don't give in to temptation to add frivolous information in order to evenly fill the page.

Because every word counts, write your story using action verbs whenever possible. For example, descriptions of your professional accomplishments always sound better and more accurate when described as "earned" rather than "received." These action verbs should showcase your skills and accomplishments in a way that contributes to your overall story. For example, if you list technical skills such as coding or computer programming, then your education or experience sections should indicate how you acquired those skills and what you have used them for. No matter what action verb you choose, make sure you resist the urge to repeatedly use the same one to describe your experience.

Descriptions of your experience should also quantify your impact. Have you led a team? Great, specify how many people. Have you managed a budget? Awesome, include how much and any other attendant responsibilities, such as fundraising or grant writing. Other common quantifiable metrics include the size of your caseload, the number of cases you have resolved successfully, the number of motions you have argued, the number of times you have testified in front of the legislature or government agency, the number of campaigns run, the number of reports you have authored, and the number of bills you were key to passing (or defeating). Quantifying your experience and accomplishments is especially important while you are in roles earlier in your career, such as a staff attorney or assistant public defender. Hiring managers will likely have a general sense of the roles and responsibilities of these positions, so it is your job to stand out from the crowd by emphasizing the competencies and achievements that demonstrate that your staff attorney experience has equipped you to be the preferred candidate for your next opportunity and rise above the rest. Remember, every word counts. Not every aspect of your experience will be quantifiable, but you should lean into bolstering your experience with these figures whenever possible.

USE PLAIN ENGLISH

It is very tempting to use jargon to display your knowledge or to sound more experienced when talking to an employer. Let's face it, we think big, complicated, or fancy words make us sound smart. Let me disabuse you of that notion. First, reviewers can often tell when you right-clicked and substituted a "big word" (synonym); it rarely looks or reads naturally. Moreover, there is a chance that your audience is not primed for such jargon or complicated terminology. While it is sometimes the case that the person doing the hiring will personally review résumés, in many situations there is a common hiring manager or assistant who may screen résumés for the person who actually makes hiring decisions or who is overall responsible for the process. There are no guarantees that another attorney, yet alone an attorney with expertise in your area, will be reviewing your materials. This is why it is imperative that you know your audience and write clearly, avoiding technical language or jargon, acronyms, or any other "inside baseball" talk. In general, nothing in your résumé should require a reviewer to Google it to understand. Writing in plain English can also let a potential employer or hiring manager know you are able to communicate clearly to clients and communities.

However, like most rules, there is an exception. If while doing your research you notice that a potential employer uses certain acronyms or jargon, it may be appropriate to include those acronyms or technical terms in your materials that are relevant to the position you are applying to. For example, if a position description uses "community lawyering" throughout the position announcement, it may be strategic to mention it in your résumé (or cover letter). Doing so may indicate to an interviewer or hiring manager that you have done your research about the company and position and are competent in the skill/area. Keep in mind, this exception to using plain English should be just that: an exception. It is likely most appropriate for a second job post-law school and not an entry-level position, as first jobs likely won't expect you to have experience in anything of consequence. Always use your best judgment.

AVOID ADJECTIVES

Over the years I have seen law students and recent graduates use adjectives to describe their experiences. For example, one young attorney's résumé read, "Expertly counseled clients on matters ranging from traffic to child support to bankruptcy." The problem? They were rather fresh out of law school, let alone experienced on multiple subject matters. Avoid being laughed out of the pool during the review process and leave the editorializing and subjective assessments of the quality of your experience to the reviewer or hiring committee. As previously discussed, starting with action verbs lets a reviewer know what you have accomplished; the only thing that adjectives add is a self-assessment of how well you think you have done it. While it is tempting to say that you "effectively managed" a project or "accurately reviewed" documents for filing, leave that out. No one will likely ever say that they were mediocre in their job, and all an employer wants to know at this point is whether you have a particular skill set or not. Leave value judgments of the quality of your skill set for the reviewer of your application, your interview, or references.

DESCRIPTION TO EMPLOYMENT LENGTH RATIO

There is an aspect to résumé reviewing that is visual, but it has to align with the experience so as not to create cognitive dissonance in the reviewer. There should be balance in the amount of real estate you dedicate to talking about your experience in a given position and some parity between the length of your description and the amount of time you worked there. It makes little sense to devote the same amount of space to a summer internship that you would to a place where you worked for three years. If you are using a paragraph format, for example, it is acceptable to dedicate three lines to the descriptions of permanent positions. However, in this format I strongly discourage using more than four lines to describe any particular position. As a general rule of thumb, I suggest keeping a summer or semester description to less than two lines (or two bullets of one line each), things you did for at least a year on three lines, and a max of four lines for a specific position. This can vary with your experience over time, and there are exceptions. For example, if you were at a place for six years and have been promoted, it may make sense to possibly dedicate four lines to each position. Use your best judgment.

When crafting résumés, I have observed that law students, especially, are often inclined to include every single task or assignment they completed at a job. This is a futile effort. I guarantee you that not every task in your past position is relevant to your future opportunity. Remember, you need to be able to speak intelligently about everything on your résumé. Make it easy on yourself by not including too much information or extraneous information. It should also go without saying that you should avoid including exaggerated (or false) information as well. An accurate, pithy résumé will take you a lot further than a verbose, lengthy one.

YOUR FORMAT SHOULD KEEP YOUR AUDIENCE ENGAGED AND FOCUSED

In chapter 4 we discussed the importance of knowing your audience. This knowledge should also inform your decisions on style and formatting. Though the profession is shifting, the norms of legal résumés and cover letters have not moved as quickly. Part of knowing your audience is recognizing that members of the hiring committee may have more traditional expectations of your application materials. While I wish it were otherwise, the reality is that it is best to stick to the basics of a more traditional format. Remember, your single goal at the application stage is to get an interview. Reviewers often have to go through stacks and stacks of résumés, figuratively speaking. In general, the public interest landscape is not known for its cutting-edge recruiting. Even when applications come in online through an applicant system, software can be clunky on the back end, so simplistic formatting can help to make sure your content is processed properly. Moreover, not every organization has software for managing the hiring process. It is not uncommon for reviewers to print application materials for review. For these reasons you should be mindful of your layout and make content and formatting decisions that make a reviewer's job as easy as possible. Knowing this, it makes complete sense to want to stand out, but there is such a thing as standing out in a bad way.

Let me give you a few tips. Don't style your résumé in a way that is distracting or makes a reviewer's job harder than it already is. Your résumé should have a balance of text and white space, as dense (or small) text can be extremely hard to read. This means staying away from multiple fonts and colors, and avoiding mixing serif and sans serif fonts. While it is commonplace to use bold, italics, or underlining to emphasize certain aspects of the résumé, using a variety of fonts and styles can make your résumé look like it was shoddily put together by someone without a command of standard formatting functions in word processing software. Traditionally, legal résumés only utilized black text, but it is becoming more common to see lawyers use one color to offset the content while sticking to a more traditional font. While serif fonts such as Times New Roman or Garamond are common for the industry, you may choose to explore a sans serif font for readability purposes. Once again, a part of this is knowing your audience. If you are applying to an organization that advocates for people with disabilities such as dyslexia or visual disabilities, then you should consider using a sans serif font in a size and type that is specifically accessible to that audience.

BULLETS OR PARAGRAPHS?

In terms of formatting, you can choose between using paragraphs or bullets to construct your experience. There are pros and cons to both, but once you choose a format, commit to it and do not mix the two styles. Résumés utilizing paragraph format are common in the legal field. They are useful when your experience can best be described in connected sentences representing responsibilities or accomplishments that build off one another. A paragraph format makes the best use of space because you can maximize the number of words that you can get on a line. Whatever you do, do not switch back and forth from bullets to paragraphs on your résumé. This is chaotic to a reviewer and rarely accomplishes what you think it does.

I'm not aware of any hard data on this, but I come across bulleted résumé formats less often in the legal field when compared to other fields. However, it is still acceptable and will not raise many eyebrows if you decide to format your résumé in this manner. To be sure, there are times when it may, in fact, be strategic to represent your experience using bullets. A bulleted format can be useful when you want to highlight concrete, yet distinct, aspects of your experience. Using bullets can also be strategic if you want to make sure that certain action verbs jump off the page to catch a reviewer's attention. It may also make sense if you are a law student with little professional experience, as bullets can help to elongate a résumé and be formatted in a way that is elegant and balances white space. Whichever format you choose will be fine, but you should always test out different résumé formats to see what works best before you commit. The format that works best for you may also change throughout the course of your career as you gain more skills and experience.

Federal Résumés

Like with other opportunities, if you are applying for a federal job you will need to tailor your résumé to fit the task. Job descriptions for federal positions include detailed qualifications that inform a job seeker what they need to demonstrate they satisfy the qualifications for various levels at which the position is slated. When you decide you are interested in the position, you should do a crosswalk of your résumé with the description. If you notice any gaps and you have the experience, you will need to update your résumé with the details to demonstrate it. (It should go without saying that if you are missing some of the requisite experience, you should seek out opportunities where you can acquire those skills.) The details required to demonstrate you meet the qualifications often include a summary, direct contact information (i.e., your current address and the addresses of past positions), and, if you are a current employee of the federal government, should include details such as your GS classification and the number of hours you work per week. Moreover, these résumés tend to follow a paragraph format to capture all of the requisite information. This is why federal résumés are often upwards of four pages.

REMEMBER, YOUR RÉSUMÉ IS THE PHYSICAL MANIFESTATION OF YOUR BRAND

First and foremost, your résumé is where you can first showcase your mastery of basic skills in the application process, such as your grasp of the English language and the use of Microsoft (MS) Word, or similar word processing software. Of law student and young attorney résumés with a skills section, almost all list MS Word. This is often unnecessary, as the résumé is the stage where you can let this competency speak for itself. This means that as you craft your résumé with a designated header it should not be formatted using tab and space bar commands. Instead, your résumé should be formatted with MS Word's (or other word processor's) formatting tools and settings. Moreover, the header on your résumé and cover letter should match. Another way to demonstrate your competency with MS Word is by using reasonably sized margins that are no larger than one inch and no smaller than a half-inch. (Remember, your résumé should have white space.)

Note: If you have a skills section, you actually do not need to include obvious skills. If it were the 1990s, or even the early 2000s, perhaps listing Microsoft Word as a skill would be unique because many workplaces were still transitioning to being computerized. In today's world, computer literacy and a proficiency in MS Word is expected. However, if you are going to list it as a skill then you must demonstrate your proficiency, and that starts with a well-formatted résumé.

TAILORING THE RÉSUMÉ TO YOUR SITUATION

Many law students and recent law school graduates ask whether they should lead their résumé with their education or their experience. In true lawyer fashion, the answer is: it depends. If you are a current law student, you should always lead with your education when you apply to legal jobs. Generally, recent law graduates (zero to three years from graduation) should lead with their education unless there is an extremely compelling reason not to. For example, a compelling reason to lead with your experience instead of your education may include the receipt of a presidential appointment or an extremely prestigious post-graduate fellowship. Even if you aren't a very recent law school graduate, you may decide to lead your résumé with your education if you attended a top-tier law school and, knowing your audience, you are aware that your target employer cares about that particular type of credential (as, unfortunately, many employers do). Leading with your education may also make sense if a hiring manager has stated they are looking to hire from a particular alumni network. If you have that information, you should use it to your advantage. After all, the goal is to get noticed and get an interview.

WHAT IF I AM NEW TO THE LAW, BUT NOT NEW TO THE WORKFORCE?

If you are a part-time law student looking to transition jobs in your current career, this may not apply to you. Part-time law students who work full-time in another field, or law students who are transitioning from another career, may decide to kick off their résumé with their experience. For example, someone holding a Ph.D. in the natural sciences (e.g., chemistry or biology) may want to lead with that experience if they are seeking a job practicing environmental law or in other science-forward attorney positions.

After your first post-law school position, or approximately three years of significant experience, you can consider leading with your experience section. However, there is one exception to this general rule where you may want to lead with your experience even if you are a fairly recent graduate, and this is if your experience is better than your education. Truthfully, this analysis makes me a bit uneasy because it represents much of the problem with elitist gatekeeping in the profession. However, the reality is that people place more value on elite (T-14) or well-known law schools, and the nonprofit and public interest industry is saturated with graduates from these institutions, especially in leadership. If you attended an unaccredited law school, for example, but have solid internship experience and a clerkship, you may want to lead with your experience and highlight certain aspects sure to grab your reader's attention. Similarly, if you know that a potential opportunity is looking for specific experience or skills you possess, then you should lead with that unique experience (and highlight it in detail in your cover letter!).

UNFORTUNATELY, WHEN IT COMES TO PUBLIC INTEREST EMPLOYMENT, CREDENTIALS AND PEDIGREE REALLY MATTER

There is an overrepresentation of lawyers who attended T-14 or other elite law schools. Interestingly enough, I have seen hiring managers and committees place an emphasis on law school rankings and the prestige of undergraduate institutions in organizations even when those managers or members of hiring committees did not attend them. (You may be thinking that this makes no sense, but this is how gatekeeping functions in practice to keep "elite" institutions and organizations "elite" and "prestigious.") Part of the task is to get in the door, and to do that you need to know your audience and communicate in their language. If your audience is partial to elite law schools and you attended one, it may help your candidacy to lead with your education.

Many law students and young attorneys arrive at becoming a public interest attorney as a second career. If you are transitioning into law from a different field, it can make sense to either lead with your education or your experience. Kicking off your résumé with your education can be a clear signal of a career pivot and show an employer you are looking to take your career in a different direction. One scenario where this makes sense is if your past career is, on its face, not neatly aligned with the career you are pursuing. Leading your résumé with your education if you are entering law as a second career may also make sense if you are looking to use your law degree to amplify your experience and take it to a different level. For example, if you worked as a paralegal at a national legal advocacy nonprofit prior to law school and are now looking to launch your legal career as an attorney at a similar organization, starting with your education can immediately establish that you have both the familiarity with the organization and the work, as well as the credentials to move to that next level. Conversely, someone in this same position may decide to lead with their experience if that experience unequivocally establishes their ability to excel in the position. These decisions are more art than science and should be decided on a case-by-case basis considering both your previous experience and the positions to which you are aspiring.

Regardless of whether you decide to lead with your experience, lead with your education, or rotate as you tailor your résumé, always make sure your formatting is consistent and that you put each section in reverse chronological order.

One Page or Two?

Law students and young attorneys often ask whether their résumé should be one page or two. As a law student there is almost zero reason why your résumé should be more than one page. As mentioned previously, with the exception of federal résumés, I strongly encourage people with less than ten years of solid, relevant experience to keep their résumé to one page. A two-page résumé is inevitable after acquiring a certain level of experience, and this level usually comes after being in the field for a decade. Regardless of length, each section should meaningfully contribute to the story of you and make the case as to why you are the candidate a reviewer is looking for. With two pages you should be able to demonstrate your skill acquisition over time (i.e., the 1 + 1 approach). Remember, your goal is to highlight what you've done and paint a picture of what you can do. Just like using big words does not make you smarter, a longer résumé does not make you the preferred candidate; it is all about content and substance. You should never be listing experience for the sake of listing it.

CONVEYING MISSION AND VALUES

Public interest employers are often looking for candidates who are committed to their mission. Indeed, alignment with an organization's mission is often incorporated into the job announcement. On your résumé the sections that most help to convey your alignment–that is, your personal mission and values–are your education and experience sections, as well as any section pertaining to service, volunteerism, or extracurricular activities. While in school you may have taken certain classes or chosen to participate in extracurriculars or student groups that aligned with your passion, interests, or values. This participation can propel you into internships, externships, clinics, or clerkships in areas that embody that mission. It may also propel you to volunteer positions or service opportunities that continue to demonstrate your commitment to a cause or mission.

If you have any experience working for, or volunteering with, organizations with similar missions to your target employer, include it. As you are describing this experience it may be strategic to dedicate a bit more space to discuss your achievements and impact. If this experience was gained through regular employment, you should discuss it in your experience section. Conversely, you can simply list it on your résumé and then use your cover letter to highlight these achievements or impact there. If your relevant experience is a volunteer position, you should list the organization in the volunteer or service section of your résumé. Because this section does not have space for descriptions, the best approach is to cross-reference this experience in your cover letter.

Unconventional or Controversial Experience

People often wonder whether they should list certain experiences or activities that may have been controversial or that they think may put their candidacy in a certain light. As passionate people committed to the public interest, it is not uncommon for law students and young attorneys to take part in organizations or support causes that may be controversial in nature. This is especially true in these polarizing political times. Law students and young lawyers must decide how much of themselves, including their identity and personal beliefs, they want to bring to their résumés. For example, do you want to include your participation in the student affiliate of the National LGBTQ+ Bar Association, which may inform a potential employer of your gender or sexuality? Should you include activities (e.g., South Asian Bar Association) that give insight into your race or ethnicity? What about those that indicate your religion or immigration status? Political beliefs? Each of these require a similar calculation of whether the potential benefits of inclusion outweigh the risks of turning off a potential reviewer. On the one hand, there are many activities we participate in or organizations we join or support that are a critical piece of our identity or belief system, and the thought of downplaying or concealing that may be a nonstarter for many law students or young attorneys. If you have done your research and know your audience, it is possible that including these types of things will signal to hiring managers or committees about the type of colleague you will be and common interests you may share. On the other hand, there are also aspects of our lives and identities we may not want to shout about from the mountaintops. Just as there are reasons to include such experience, there are also reasons to exclude it. A reviewer of your résumé may read it and be distracted by your beliefs at the expense of your skills. Or a reviewer, through their own bias, may interpret certain participation as out of alignment with their organization's values and summarily discard your application. Much of this analysis will be personal and specific to you, but you should be intentional with each application.

Moreover, interviews are a two-way street. Just as an employer is interviewing you, you are also interviewing your potential employer. An applicant should always question whether they want to work for a place that may be turned off, or fetishize, your identity and experience. If you want to see how an organization "walks the walk" on equity and inclusion, or a commitment to other values, then you may consider including these types of background information or experiences as a test. If you make it to the interview process, you can gain insight into how they value those aspects of your experience, and identity, and use it to make a more informed decision as to whether you want to work there. At the end of the day whether to include these experiences is a personal decision, but one that should be made with the knowledge of how such experiences may land on a potential employer.

If you decide to include unconventional or controversial experience, it is important to know how to discuss the experience and what skills you developed. If you worked for a controversial organization as a full-time job it will be important to describe that work in the experience section. When doing this, you should emphasize your accomplishments, measurable impact, quantifiable outcomes, or the broad-based skill that you developed. You are telling a story of your skills that needs to provide a counternarrative to someone who may be inclined to overly focus on where you gained your experience, as opposed to your level of mastery. Other sections that may include experiences with controversial organizations or those organizations that give sharp insights into your identity will likely be located in the education section on your résumé (e.g., student organizations), in a section on volunteer experience, or in a section on professional affiliations or service to the profession. The inclusion of these experiences on your résumé, demonstrating that you have built relevant skills to the position you are applying for, should be complemented by your cover letter, allowing you to provide more color and context. A focus on your skills and demonstrable outcomes, and how they prepare you for the current opportunity, will be critical to a successful narrative for your candidacy.

CONFRONTING ANTI-BLACK CAREER ADVICE

Anti-Blackness, or the systemic devaluation and marginalization of Black people both overtly and through covert structural and systemic racism, permeates American institutions and structures. The workplace is no different. Anti-Blackness has not only informed workplace culture and norms, but also permeated career advice about how to enter that culture and be a "fit." When considering career advice it is important to name and acknowledge anti-Blackness as a historical feature, especially given the fact that being a Black attorney has historically meant navigating traditionally white institutions and power structures, and Black attorneys remain only five percent of the profession.[1] There is a never-ending trove of advice on respectability and appearances—don't wear hoops, braids, locs, afros, "frizzy" (read: naturally kinky or curly) hair—that is anti-Black in nature. It is also not unheard of to hear advice that people of color should use an initial in place of their ethnic-sounding first name so they aren't prejudged, or conversely, not to use an initial for that same reason, such as when places are looking for "diverse" hires. The equally difficult reality is that a lot of this advice is further perpetuated by Black attorneys and attorneys of color who have often adopted these strategies as a coping mechanism to survive in these traditionally white environments and make space for those of us who came after.

I, too, have received advice from older, well-meaning Black professionals that I shouldn't have a bunch of experience on my résumé that makes me look like a "Black" candidate. My résumé was once reviewed by a colleague who highlighted everything about my résumé that fit the bill of the "Black" candidate: majoring in Africana Studies, leadership positions in Ethos (a Black women's student organization at Wellesley College), a graduate degree in African-American Studies, service on a board that served inner-city or urban areas, co-founding a Black alumni organization, participating in professional development fellowships or programs for Black women and professionals of color, affiliations with organizations with the word "urban" in the title, and the like. Their concern was twofold: first, that this experience signals that I am a Black candidate, which can lead a biased reviewer to discard my application; and second, an employer may read my passion for Black people as an apathy toward others. In the end, they recommended that I cut these experiences from my résumé.

[1] American Bar Association, *ABA Profile of the Legal Profession: 2020* (2020) https://www.americanbar.org/content/dam/aba/administrative/news/2020/07/potlp2020.pdf (last visited July 13, 2021).

Note: Not for nothing, I have found the latter concern about the way a potential employer can perceive your passion to be somewhat valid and something to consider when seeking new opportunities. You cannot control how people interpret your passion and experience, all you can do is make it as clear as possible. This is why knowing your audience and being clear about your value is so important.

This also wasn't the first time I had received this type of advice. As a woman I've been told to wear a pantsuit to be taken seriously by men and older colleagues, to buy a wedding ring to be taken seriously as a woman in the statehouse and protect myself from predatory men, and, contradictorily, to not wear a wedding ring so that people won't second-guess my commitment to the job as I rise in seniority. As a Black woman I have been told to straighten my hair, take out my nose ring, don't wear gold, don't wear hoop earrings, don't wear fake nails, and the like. The clear message was that I needed to get into the door, and that it was necessary to make these adjustments to increase my chances. The thing is, once you have made it into the door, the adjustments and accommodations never stop there. I have seen countless Black attorneys (and other professionals) be socialized into being overly formal so as to be "professional" and nonthreatening, only to be penalized for it during performance reviews and told that they were "not personable" or "not a fit" for the environment.

The misconception that law students and young attorneys often have is that this advice only applies to corporate attorneys or those in the private sector; this could not be further from the truth. Many public interest organizations were not created with Black people or people of color (and, sometimes, women) in mind, and were especially not made for Black women and other women of color. This lack of inclusive origin can be compounded by the corporate cultures adopted by many of these organizations. Historically, integration has meant placing Black and Brown people in white environments, and that is still what much of diversity and inclusion efforts amount to in organizations today.

To be fair, this type of advice is outdated, and certainly not as common as it once was. Nonetheless, it is important to mention because this type of advice is out there and even if people have learned not to give this advice that doesn't mean they no longer believe that young attorneys should heed it. To be clear, there are people who think Black attorneys and attorneys of color should keep a portion of themselves home to fit into a work environment. If an employer demands changes in appearance or demeanor, you should explore whether those demands extend to the type of work you are able to do and the way in which you are able to do it. For example, is this an organization where you can name racism in the workplace or where you have to stick to talking about class and vague notions of inequality? I strongly encourage any law student or young attorney to research and seriously consider whether they want to work for an organization that requires they contort who they are to fit the mold of who and what an organization thinks they should be. This is an especially important consideration at the outset because it will inform the rest of your journey and directly relate to personal fulfillment.

7

The Rest of the Package

As your career takes off and you seek out more senior positions, employers are often looking to see whether a candidate can be trusted to deliver quality work product autonomously the first time. A solid application package is the first test of this ability. This is why you can't just nail your résumé, but you need to nail the entirety of your application package. This chapter will cover the primary complementary material that comprises an application package: the cover letter, LinkedIn profile, and writing sample. I will discuss approaches to cover letters when applying for positions under different circumstances, such as for an internship, an internal promotion, or a "cold call" application online.

THE COVER LETTER

Cover letter writing is an art. While cover letter writing is a form of technical writing, it is more of a pitch where you have less than a page to capture a reviewer and let them know that you are the total package they have been looking for (i.e., the preferred candidate). The cover letter needs to demonstrate your interest, provide an overview of your experience, and leave a reviewer with enough confidence in your skill set that they want to learn more. Your cover letter should be about you but written with your audience—the employer, hiring manager, fellowship committee, and so on—in mind. As you are writing, consider their needs and write in your target audience's language. This means writing in plain English but weaving in technical terms as appropriate to communicate your qualifications. Regardless of how you are targeting your audience, your cover letter should be well-written.

COVER LETTER WRITING IS AN ART

You have less than a page to capture a reviewer and let them know you are the preferred candidate they have been seeking.

The cover letter needs to:

- Demonstrate your interest
- Provide an overview of your experience
- Leave a reviewer with enough confidence in your skill set that they want to learn more

Your cover letter should reflect the needs of the target employer. One thing you should try to determine is whether their needs are short term or long term. An employer with short-term needs may be less concerned with a person's ties to a geographic region than one with long-term needs. Similarly, an employer with longer-term needs may be more amenable to a flexible start date than one who has immediate needs and is looking for someone now. You should also try to assess who your audience's ideal candidate is. Understanding their preferred candidate can help refine your pitch. Similarly, an employer with short-term needs may be more concerned with an applicant's current skills, as opposed to what they can learn down the line.

Note: Your cover letter should utilize the same font and size as your résumé. The margins should also be the same size, with justified margins. This is because you are trying to impress the hiring manager and demonstrate your proficiency in delivering professional work products. You would never submit companion documents in completely different formats to a client, so you should not do that here. Moreover, uniform formatting makes your materials easier on the eyes for a person to review.

Use a Heading

A heading on a cover letter is a useful convention that, when done properly, can leave a positive impression of your brand and professionalism on an employer. A good heading lets an employer know your name and qualifications (e.g., Marcus Blake, Esq.); you would be amazed at how many headings fail to communicate this basic information. Your heading should also include contact information and a general location. I also strongly encourage law students and young attorneys to include a link to your LinkedIn profile, though it is not required. The heading should also mirror the one used on your résumé in terms of font, style, and information provided. This may seem like an inconsequential formatting hack, but a bold, sleek heading on your materials can bolster an employer's impression of you and strengthen your brand.

You may be wondering whether to include your address in the heading. The answer to this will depend on your audience. Evidence suggests that discrimination against candidates residing in stigmatized communities is a regular occurrence. It is logical that candidates may seek to improve their chances by excluding information that may trigger an employer's bias, especially if there are other items on their résumé that may reveal their race, gender, sexuality, or other aspect that can form the basis of discrimination. Luckily, conventions of headings for résumés have evolved a bit, to the point that an exact street address is not required. So, while people have largely stopped including a street address, many do still include a city and state, and there are a few reasons to consider doing so. One such reason is to demonstrate to your audience that you are familiar with, and have ties to, a particular community or geographic region. This may be strategic if you are applying to an organization that is located

SAMPLE HEADINGS

JONATHAN CASTRO, ESQ.
jonathancastro@email.me | Oakland, CA • (555) 555-5555

Cherish
Baker-Williams

New York
(555) 555-5555
cherishbw@email.me
www.linkedin.com/in/cherish-baker-williams

Nanette Champlain | Esq., M.A.
Houston, TX | (c) 555-5555 | Nanette.c@email.me

in or serves that particular community. Another reason to include a general location in your heading is to signal to an employer that you are local and can start right away without requiring relocation assistance; this is especially important if the opportunity is not remote and the employer requires any time in the office. Depending on the opportunity, this decision to include your general location in your header may be strategically expedient.

Keep in mind, headings (and résumé formatting more generally) are a brand management strategy. A bold heading and a regional connection can combine to leave a great first impression on a reviewer, signaling to them that you may be the preferred candidate. Round out the top of your cover letter by addressing the hiring manager and avoid writing "Dear Hiring Manager" to the greatest extent possible.

THE FIRST PARAGRAPH: DEMONSTRATE INTEREST

I have seen more than my fair share of cover letters that started with "My name is _____ and I am applying to the _____ position at _(company)_." Once upon a time, I, too, wasted precious space by stating my name at the beginning of my cover letter—under the heading where it was already included. Even worse, I used to use my cover letter to parrot my résumé. This is a common mistake I have also seen law students and young attorneys make more times than I care to admit. This is such a missed opportunity! The reality is, there is not enough space in the cover letter for any redundant information, whether it be your name or other identical details culled from your résumé.

In order to demonstrate interest, consider utilizing the first paragraph to pitch your employer. In chapter 5 we briefly mentioned the topic of summary captions on résumés. While I maintain that it is not a good use of space on a résumé, the opening paragraph of a cover letter is an appropriate place to include such a statement. One strategy to craft a summary statement that can open your resume is to organize it about a common theme; this is relatively straightforward for those whose career path has been relatively linear. As you advance in your career you may find that a short summary statement will be easier to craft, as your brand will be more refined. Another strategy is to orient your statement about the accumulation of transferrable skills; this strategy can be particularly helpful if you have either seemingly unrelated experience or transitioned into the law from another field. Using transferable skills as a thematic scheme for your cover letter can help move your audience through parts of your background that are nonlinear or not clearly related. Remember, your cover letter should be both compelling and to the point.

THE BODY: DEMONSTRATE YOU ARE THE PREFERRED CANDIDATE

Your cover letter should complement your résumé, not duplicate it. Taken together, your résumé and cover letter tell a story, and the conclusion that reviewers should draw from that story should be that you are what they have been looking for; that is, the preferred candidate. Your résumé details your career path and showcases your skills. Your cover letter bolsters your story as a candidate by providing the narrative that links all your experience together and communicates your alignment with the company and its mission. Your only goal is to leave an employer with the impression that you are the preferred candidate and a no-brainer to interview (and hire!). To make this happen, you need to craft a narrative that speaks to both an organization's needs and values while weaving in concrete supporting details about your skills and track record of success. In other words, tell your story in their language.

There are strategies you can use while writing to bridge the difference between your past experience and your next opportunity. As you discuss your past experience you should make sure you organize your cover letter in a way that addresses the experiences most relevant to the new position first. To this end, when referring to current or past experience you should generally do so in the past tense. Your cover letter should also speak to a potential employer in their own language, using keywords (i.e., the company's lingo from the website or job description) that are relevant to the position you are targeting, but remember, try striking a balance by not using too many buzz words or too much jargon. Where you cannot bridge your experience using the organization's lingo, try to use language that is more generic in nature; this will help to downplay differences between past positions you have held and the one you are seeking. This strategy can be particularly useful when your target position is in a different field or if you are changing subfields or practice settings. For example, policy counsels don't tend to manage a caseload, but those skills can be discussed as relevant to juggling priorities in a legislative session. It is critical that you explicitly state the connections between past experience and the present position and never leave it up to your reader to figure it out for themselves.

STRATEGIES TO BRIDGE PAST EXPERIENCE WITH A FUTURE OPPORTUNITY

1. Talk about your most relevant experience first.
2. Keep it short; use one page max.
3. Use the organization's lingo but try not to sound like a buzz word robot.

KEEP IT TIGHT

The final paragraph of your cover letter should drive home your qualifications. A shorter rephrasing of your summary statement from the opening paragraph can be used to accomplish this goal. After that, wrap up by thanking your audience and welcoming additional conversation. In general, your cover letter should not be longer than a single page. Only on the rare occasion should your cover letter ever flow onto a second page, and you should use your judgment to determine whether this is appropriate. For example, if you are applying to a position internally and want to use your cover letter to tell a story, you may take liberty with the length of the cover letter knowing that your target audience (i.e., your current colleagues) will likely take more time with your application out of respect for you. But again, even if you are in this situation, you should ask yourself whether that is the best use of their time. To conform with traditional expectations and show respect for the sheer volume of résumés and cover letters received by hiring managers, you should stick to one page.

> In this rare situation—where you are going for an internal promotion—there may be more leeway in terms of the length of your materials. However, just because you can go longer doesn't mean that you should. While your colleagues may read more information about you, your cover letter is not necessarily the best place to drop that information. Instead, you should develop a plan to strategically seed the information that you want them to know over time. This plan is particularly important since you will likely need the support and advocacy of your colleagues if your application is going to be successful.

AVOIDING COMMON COVER LETTER PITFALLS

- Typos and grammatical errors
- Irregular fonts or inconsistent formatting
- Regurgitating information already included in the résumé
- Failing to tell a story bringing your experience to life
- Failing to communicate mission or doing so in an inauthentic way

YOUR LINKEDIN PROFILE IS A PART OF YOUR APPLICATION PACKAGE

Let's face it, we live in an age of social media where we can now be found and researched more easily than ever. Your next employer may have an impression of you before they even open your materials. At this stage, not having a LinkedIn page is almost career malpractice, so I strongly advise law students and young attorneys to create and maintain one. This is also a free opportunity to showcase your brand and bolster your candidacy. To be clear, the advice here is to have a LinkedIn presence and use it to manage your professional brand; this does not mean you need to become a LinkedIn influencer. If the goal is to manage the information people can learn about you, sometimes less is more. Always use your best judgment in determining what you post on any social media channel, but especially LinkedIn.

Unlike your résumé, which you can tailor to different jobs and audiences, your LinkedIn page is just one profile that should reflect your combined experience in a clear, concise manner. You should use your master résumé to guide you as you create, or update, your LinkedIn profile. While many people just add on experience after experience, that is not always the best approach. As with anything, it is important to develop a strategy. I would start by thinking through the following set of sequential questions:

1. What do I want my professional reputation to be?
2. Does my current LinkedIn profile give off that impression?
3. Does my current LinkedIn profile adequately describe the skills I possess and the things I have accomplished?
4. What skills/opportunities/connections am I looking to develop? (This question should inform the sections about who can contact you and what they should contact you about. This question should also inform what next opportunities you are open to and the skills you are looking to develop.)

At this point in the book the first question should sound familiar. Your professional reputation is not to be taken lightly. Earlier I mentioned that the first part of my strategy for launching a successful public interest career is to start with yourself and envision where you want to go. You have to know where you are professionally trying to go in order to determine whether your image (and strategy) match your getting there. Understanding your destination can provide you with perspective about the journey. Use that perspective to evaluate whether your LinkedIn profile leaves the impression you need it to. An important part of this is reflecting on how you want to be known once you get there. Some people may want the reputation as the "best" of a certain type of job, such as the best public defender or the best prosecutor in a geographic region. Others may want to be known by their unique particular experience, such as the foremost authority on bail reform in New Jersey. Others may want to be recognized by their gate-opening impact, such as the first Latina judge who turned around and hired and mentored other Latinx attorneys who are now judges or in other prominent positions. Brands work best when they are known for one primary thing. No matter what you are aspiring to, your LinkedIn profile is a natural reflection point to ask whether your profile reflects the reputation you have and leaves an impression on where you can go and what you can do when you get there.

Assessing whether your LinkedIn profile gives off the impression you want it to requires going back to the fundamentals. The essence of LinkedIn is serving as a digital résumé to facilitate professional networking, so it is important to make sure your profile adequately, and accurately, describes your past experience, your interests, and the skills you have developed. With each profile view comes the opportunity to leave a curated impression on employers. The first opportunity is the headline that appears underneath your name. Many LinkedIn users choose to use their job titles (e.g., Deputy Prosecuting Attorney at Elkhart County Prosecutor's Office) or student status (e.g., 2L at University of Tennessee College of Law) as their headline. If you have a snazzy job title or unique fellowship, you may want to include that as your headline. Alternatively, you can describe your skills more broadly (e.g., Consumer Protection Attorney or Housing Justice Advocate). Regardless of what you decide, you should be aware that this headline is picked up by search engines, so more common terms can increase the likelihood of your profile being picked up in a search. Once your LinkedIn profile gives the vibe that aligns with the destination, you can fine-tune your profile, checking that the supporting details are adequate. This means making sure your skills are listed and any accomplishments or commendations are clearly denoted.

Draw Your Reader in with a Succinct Summary

The second opportunity to craft an impression is in your summary, also known as the about section. While I vehemently disagree with including a summary on your résumé, LinkedIn is a place where a dynamic summary is appropriate and can set the tone for how a person perceives your page. The summary is the opportunity to marry your passion and experience in a compelling narrative tailored for future opportunities. For example, someone seeking a stakeholder engagement or community lawyering position job can craft a summary that showcases their personality and highlights their people skills. Similarly, someone seeking a position requiring complex litigation skills can craft a summary highlighting their qualifying experience and matters resolved. Like with your cover letter, you can either craft a summary that is connected by a common theme or you can craft one where transferrable skills serve as the through line. Either way, utilize this opportunity to draw in your audience and make them curious enough to want to learn about (i.e., scroll through) the rest of your skills.

You should always include a link to your LinkedIn profile in your email signature. Doing so will not only make it easier for a potential employer to find you but can potentially discourage them from conducting an initial Google search. Such a search will inevitably yield results that are out of your control, so providing more information to satisfy an employer's curiosity can be beneficial. The strategy is to use your LinkedIn profile as a way to feed a target employer (or recruiter) relevant information to curate the impression you want to leave them with. After a hiring manager has received your application materials, a LinkedIn search should confirm their first impression and secure an interview.

TIP: WHEN CRAFTING A LINKEDIN PROFILE, ASK YOURSELF THE FOLLOWING SERIES OF QUESTIONS:

1. What do I want my professional reputation to be?
2. Does my current LinkedIn profile give off that impression?
3. Does my current LinkedIn profile adequately describe the skills I possess and the things I have achieved?
4. What skills/opportunities/connections am I looking to develop?

SUBMITTING THE APPLICATION

When it comes to the act of submitting the final application package it will likely be in one of two ways: online through an applicant tracking system or emailing your materials to a designated contact or email address. In this day and age where applications are rarely sent via mail or hand delivered, it is important to know that mass applying; that is, submitting a multitude of applications to as many jobs as possible or submitting multiple applications to the same employer, is generally frowned upon. A job search is not a numbers game, and should not be treated as such. While it is okay to occasionally "shoot your shot" it is not a great strategy, and certainly not advice that, in and of itself, leads to a successful and fulfilling career.

When submitting your application, one way to build and maintain your brand is to make sure your actions match your words. Each step in the job search is an opportunity to demonstrate your follow-through, and this includes submitting the application. Employers want an employee who can pay attention to detail, and submitting an application the way an employer wants is exactly how you showcase that quality. If a job posting provides specific instructions about how to submit the application and what to include, FOLLOW THE INSTRUCTIONS. This may seem obvious, but so many people fail to do so. You've sent one email application, so you've sent them all, right? Wrong! If there is an email address to direct your application to, direct your materials there with either the requested subject heading or an otherwise straightforward subject line (e.g., Staff Attorney Application – Your Name). The preferred candidate always follows simple instructions.

Submitting your application is also an opportunity to showcase your ability to take initiative. Many job announcements include the name of the hiring manager or human resources (HR) contact; when this happens, you should use it. If there is no name included, researching who to address an emailed application to when there is no name mentioned (e.g., hr@potentialopportunity.com) can also demonstrate to an employer that you are diligent and detail-oriented. To the extent that it is possible, try to avoid using "Dear Hiring Manager" and try to find who to address your application to. However, if you do this it is important that you address it to the right person. Just as easily as proactive research can leave a positive impression on a potential employer, shoddy research resulting in an inaccurately addressed or misdirected application can undermine your efforts at a first impression. Being the preferred candidate means knowing your audience, and that starts with correctly addressing the application.

A General Note on Emailing Résumés

In general, it is not usually a good idea to send your résumé along unsolicited. It is likely that you will be sending your résumé along via email in scenarios other than in the job application context. Such scenarios may include following up with a contact you met either at a networking event or via another connection, responding to a recruiter who has reached out, reaching out prior to an informational interview, updating mentors or career services advisors, or forwarding it to someone who has previously agreed to review your résumé. It is important to craft your email in an effective way in those circumstances, too.

By this point it should go without saying, but always keep it professional. This includes writing an effective subject line. An effective subject line informs the recipient of the subject, the ask, and, if applicable, any timeline. Again, if your recipient has provided any instructions, you should follow them. While it is tempting to use common subjects like "touching base" or "following up" with little else, these subject headings tend not to be effective for two reasons. First, they are so commonly used they are easy to be overlooked, especially if your recipient doesn't know you. More importantly, they lack specificity and do not provide your recipient with any information on what you are asking and how to prioritize it. Instead, try to use a subject that makes clear why you are emailing and how you are connected, such as "Wellesley Alum requesting informational interview." Similarly, if you are connected to your recipient through a friend but you have not yet met, you can try, "Following up on Alex's introduction, this is Maya" or something similar. In this post-COVID virtual world there have been many opportunities to attend online lectures, webinars, book talks, CLEs, and other virtual panels and events where participants may invite the audience to reach out to them. In these situations, you may try an email with a subject line such as, "Following up from the tech and civil liberties CLE—Cherise Whiteside." If you are continuing the conversation with a colleague who you interacted with in a virtual chat, breakout group, or other more personal virtual interaction, you can potentially say something along the lines of, "Let's continue the conversation from the Under the Blacklight series." Whatever the specific situation, your goal is to anchor your subject line in something that catches your recipient's interest and makes them open it in a timely manner.

Once you have written a subject heading that captures attention, it is critical that you hold their attention by keeping your message brief and to the point. Again, words are your friends, but remember, the *right* words, not just more words. Are you asking a person to review your résumé and providing them with relevant resources about the purpose of the review? Great, you should be able to ask that in less than three paragraphs (read: one). Always write considering your audience; ask yourself what they think is important and what you want them to take away from this message. You should also be mindful and realistic about the amount of time that your audience will spend on your email. A concise message should make your pitch in the first sentence and highlight your value soon after. Be sure to include any relevant timelines or next steps. Most importantly, be warm and amiable. No one appreciates aggressive or confrontational emails, even when they may have dropped the ball. A key way to remain positive is to include a genuine thank you in your message (which can also be reflected in the subject heading).

Finally, remember that these emails are often your first impression and it is on you to make it a good one. Remain professional, proofread your email, and double check to make sure all attachments are, in fact, attached. Good luck!

8

The Hiring Process

By now you are probably asking the question: *What is the actual hiring process?* Unfortunately, there is no standard hiring process. In fact, it is quite to the contrary. It is not only common for hiring processes to differ across employers but also within organizations. In this sense, mission-driven legal organizations tend to follow general trends of nonprofits; according to a 2017 study only 33 percent of nonprofits had a formal recruitment strategy.[1] Unfortunately, it is also not uncommon for legal advocacy organizations to have little or no formal HR departments or dedicated staff. In my experience, nonprofit legal organizations often refuse to make investments into HR and recruitment (or retention) strategies because they prioritize money toward fulfilling the mission. As a result, many organizations have decentralized hiring processes run by individual staff members serving as hiring managers. (Other nonhiring HR functions are often diffused across various staff members in these organizations.) Conversely, government organizations tend to have dedicated staff and clear processes for hiring, though the bureaucratic nature of these hiring processes can tend to move slowly.

The lack of dedicated staff and resources for recruitment can inevitably make hiring processes in nonprofit legal advocacy organizations

[1] https://www.nonprofithr.com/2017-nep-survey-new/#section-4.

unpredictable, except for common practices that have been ingrained into attorneys. As such, there are elements of the application process that are pretty common, such as screening calls and writing sample requirements. Many hiring managers and hiring consultants rely on a screening call with applicants. The screening call is often a short call, usually thirty minutes or less, that is both high stakes and low stakes; it is high stakes for an applicant and low stakes for an employer. Screening calls can help an employer who has received a large volume of applications to begin to narrow the pool. During these calls a hiring manager may ask about an applicant's interest in the organization in addition to questions verifying the experience necessary to qualify for the position. You should prepare for this interview by doing research on the company and specific position you are applying for. There will not be time to go extremely in depth, so you should have one or two high-level talking points ready to go. And make sure to be friendly; a constant question your future employer is asking themselves is: *Would I like to work with this person*? Remember, being the preferred candidate necessarily means being a good coworker.

QUESTIONS TO REFLECT UPON AS YOU DEVELOP YOUR TALKING POINTS

1. Why do you want this job?
2. What skills do you have that best align with this job?
3. What makes you a unique candidate?

If the screening call goes well, you may be offered an interview. This interview has traditionally been in-person but may increasingly be virtual. You should generally expect at least two interviews with at least two different members of staff. For entry-level attorney positions it is common for candidates to meet with their potential boss and colleagues who they may work closely with. Occasionally a member of senior leadership will also participate in these interviews; participation by senior leadership is much more common for more senior positions. Moreover, the interview process of smaller organizations or startups may involve meeting founders or executive directors. These interviews can vary in format, but panel interviews with members of staff are extremely common. When you are scheduling an interview, the scheduler will probably end an email by saying, "Please let me know if you have any questions." This is an invitation to respond and ask directly about the interview's format and who you should expect to be interviewed by. A good way to anticipate who may be a member of your interview panel is by looking up the organization and the staff who works on the team you are interviewing for. Research and preparation are key, and the application stage of the job search process is no different. Use the correspondence as an opportunity to leave a good impression and demonstrate you are the preferred candidate.

GETTING PAST AUTOMATED APPLICATION SYSTEMS

We are living in a computerized world, where technology is an inevitable part of the job search process. The vast majority of jobs are posted online. Moreover, there are a number of organizations that rely on technology to make their recruitment and hiring process more manageable, with many using applicant tracking systems to manage applications. With applying to jobs now being easier than ever, many companies and recruiters are using these automated systems to manage what can sometimes be hundreds or even thousands of applications, especially for entry-level positions. In what may be a growing trend, one-third of nonprofits reported using an applicant tracking system in 2017.[2] These systems are particularly helpful to address the phenomenon of mass applying, as discussed previously. As a result, these systems become critical tools for employers to filter candidate applications so that only the most "qualified" candidates

[2] https://www.nonprofithr.com/2017-nep-survey-new/#section-19.

are passed forward to the review stage by a human. However, whether an applicant is qualified or not is often less about their credentials and more about how an applicant framed their experience in their materials. This is yet another reason why intentional research and strategy for your résumé and cover letter is important.

BEWARE OF THE ANECDOTES: WHY MASS APPLYING IS BAD STRATEGY

Every so often you will hear about someone who has applied to "hundreds" of jobs and received either no callbacks or a negligible amount of interview offers. Sometimes the argument being made is that it doesn't matter whether you are qualified and that jobs are given to people they know. Other times this mass applying anecdote is used to emphasize how much effort it takes to get a job. Either way, beware of the anecdotes. When shared, the author is often making one or more assumptions, including: 1) they are the preferred candidate of each employer applied to; 2) their application package is top notch; 3) they meet most of the requirements and would be good at each of the jobs they apply for; and 4) when they receive responses, their follow-up and interview are top notch. Needless to say, these are bad assumptions. Remember, you should be tailoring your materials for each job you are applying to; people who are mass applying tend not to do this, as it would slow down the number of places they are able to apply to. If you are not tailoring your materials, you certainly are not reflecting on whether your experience matches what an employer is looking for, and your application is likely not top notch. As a result, it is rare that mass applying gets you through the initial screening to receive a callback.

> There is plenty to learn from others who have similar experiences, but make sure you critically examine anecdotes before buying into the messages.

When an employer is using an automated system, the goal is to "beat the bot," so to speak. The most effective way to do this is to identify buzz words and phrases from the job description and strategically incorporate them into your application materials. This does not mean paraphrasing bullets from the qualifications or responsibilities section of the job description; I have seen applicants do this and do not recommend it. However, the strategic deployment of certain keywords can indicate to an employer that not only do you grasp the nature of the job, but you also can clearly tie your previous experience to what you would bring to the table in this potential role. That is ultimately the message you want to send.

You may be wondering: *How do I identify buzz words in a job description*? It is a great question. Sometimes you will be able to tell by just looking, while other times you may need to read between the lines. For example, if a job description mentions "community lawyering" or "integrated advocacy" multiple times, that is an indicator it may be a keyword. Other keywords may include the practice area of the position, geographic area, or certain skills critical to successfully complete the work. The more familiar you are with an organization and the types of work they do, the easier it may be to identify the keywords. You can also cross-check the job announcement against the organization's website in order to identify keywords.

Let's face it, not all job descriptions are well written. In fact, many job descriptions are poorly written and ill conceived. Some employers throw in the kitchen sink in terms of both job responsibilities and candidate qualifications. If you read a job description and can't tell what exactly the job is, ask clarifying questions in the interview. If it sounds like an employer is actually describing the work of three people, or a list of qualities that tend not to exist in only one person, parse through that in your questions. I would encourage you to still apply, as there may be flexibility in the role for the right person. However, I encourage you to make sure that the particular role and responsibilities make sense for you and can be done in the scope of a forty-hour workweek before you accept an offer. When looking for positions, you should make sure you are set up for success, and that includes only having job responsibilities and metrics that are manageable for one person. Public interest lawyers are at particular risk of burnout because they are often expected to do too much with too few resources and too little pay. Most people who enter this area of the law are passionate about the work. That is no justification for accepting a position where the structure does not exist to support your success from the outset.

When job openings are scarce, it may be tempting to attempt shortcuts to try to "beat the bot" and help your résumé get past the automated screening. For example, I have heard people advise candidates to plant words from the job description in white font in the blank space on your résumé. No matter how tempting it is, this is a bad idea and I do not suggest that applicants do this. It is thought that this may be advantageous because the program will match the hidden words to keywords they are looking for and pass along the résumé. While the white font may be invisible to the naked eye, these automated systems aimed to grab text can sometimes pick them up in the conversion of documents into the system to send to reviewers and this additional text can end up in odd places that interrupt your intended content. You also never want your first impression to be an attempt to cheat the system; you may as well not have applied. Remember, you and your materials are your brand. You should always act in accordance with the impression you want to leave on someone and how you want people to be able to speak about you in your absence.

9

Staying on Brand Through the Interview Phase

Once you have submitted an application, the next stage of the game is staying on brand during the follow-up and through the interview phase. The waiting game starts once you submit your application. You should not expect a response from every position you apply to. This is especially so when the job market is tight, as I have heard of recent job announcements receiving as many as a few hundred applicants, with a couple having received over 1,000; this is especially true for positions allowing hybrid or remote work in a post-COVID environment. The sheer volume of applications is one reason why you need to put your best-branded foot forward when you submit your résumé and cover letter and stay on brand throughout your entire time as a candidate. However, when an employer does reach out to you, you need to be ready.

STAY ON BRAND IN YOUR COMMUNICATIONS

These days, the most likely method of communication from an employer is an email, making it extremely important to be mindful of email etiquette. Always respond in a manner that accounts for the possibility of your email being forwarded and read by an audience other than the intended recipient. When replying, your first email should always be formal and include a salutation. You should make sure you address the sender only in the ways you are invited to do so. If the person signs their full first name, that is often an indication that they prefer to be called by their full first name. For example, if a person signs their name Nicholas, do not shorten it to Nick. In the legal profession it is important to have relational skills and an attention to detail; this is yet another opportunity to demonstrate these soft skills during the application process.

When drafting emails you should also be mindful of people's pronouns. Though it is still common for people to refer to other people using "Mr." or "Ms." in formal writing, it is more important than ever to be respectful of people's pronouns, especially as a public interest attorney. Pronouns in email signatures are more common than ever. If a person has included their pronouns, you should only use the traditional salutations if they match the person's pronouns. If you are unsure of a person's pronouns, it is okay to refer to people by their first name, such as "Dear Nicholas," or similar formal greeting. Whatever you do, do not get a person's pronouns wrong, as that could send the wrong message to an employer. For example, you don't want to give an employer that fights for LGBTQ+ rights the impression that you are not an ally. Similarly, if you are including cultural competency as a feature of your personal brand, you don't want to come off as a liar because of a pronoun's faux pas. Do your research, know your audience, and be respectful to stay in the running.

THE WAITING GAME

As you pursue opportunities to acquire the skills that would make you a preferred candidate, it will not be all sunshine and rainbows, or, in this case, callbacks and job offers. It will sometimes be the case that you put yourself out there to only a lukewarm response, if any response at all. That is okay. It happens. And frankly, if you're batting 1,000 you probably aren't taking enough (read: any) risks in your search. While people often go to great lengths to say that you shouldn't compare yourself to others, I think that job seeking is an area where comparison to others is not only a helpful exercise in self-awareness but can also greatly inform your growth and development. If you have interviewed with an organization that later turns you down for a job, you should follow up with the hiring manager and ask if they have any feedback for you. After receiving this feedback, reflect on it and discuss it with a mentor to develop a plan to put the critical feedback into action. If an organization posts their staff on the website (as many organizations outside of government do), you should always look to see who got the position instead of you. Examining their bio, experiences, and skills can help you identify what you need to be competitive for the next similar opportunity. Sometimes it is easier to see how the chosen candidate aligns than it is to see how you don't. And while you are examining how the other candidate compares to the job listing, you should also look at how they differ from you. Perhaps you notice there is a blatant gap in your experience. Or perhaps the candidate selected has a professional journey you can see yourself taking. When you meet with your mentor or coach, make sure to discuss ways to either find opportunities to stretch in your current position or to explore pro bono or other volunteer or service opportunities.

WHEN SHOULD YOU FOLLOW UP?

Once you have applied it is perfectly natural to be anxious about receiving a response. There is no hard rule about follow-up communications, but you can use the job posting to develop a good strategy. For example, if a job posting says they are only responding to candidates they are moving forward to interview, you should think twice before reaching out, and if you decide to do so, you should not expect a response. However, if you have a contact at the organization, it is completely appropriate to ask them about any updates on the hiring process. You should also never reach out to a hiring manager prior to the expiration of the job posting. In general, you should wait at least two weeks after the expiration of a job posting, or a position's priority application deadline, before reaching out. For example, if a job posting closes on October 31st or has a priority application deadline but accepts applications on a rolling basis, I wouldn't reach out to follow up if you haven't heard anything before November 15th, at the earliest. Whether you follow up and how you do so may also be determined by the way you applied. If you submitted materials by email either directly to a hiring manager or to a designated email address, it is okay to reach out after a period of time. You should use your best judgment to determine how long of a period of time is appropriate. If a job has a closing date listed for the posting you should never reach out prior to the closing date; it is best to wait at least a week after any posting closes. For applications submitted via portal, it is okay to attempt to leverage your network to identify connections at the company, but I would not follow up without a personal contact. While it is disappointing to spend time and effort on an application and not hear back, following up by sending emails into the ether is probably not a productive use of time.

It is not unusual to not receive any word from an employer, including a confirmation email. There are also many situations where you will not know the outcome of a search until an announcement is made, and that's okay. It is also not unheard of for an employer to repost a position even after they have conducted interviews. If this happens, you should assume you are not in the running; do not just reapply for the position. Instead, this is the perfect opportunity to reach out and solicit feedback. If you do decide it makes sense to reapply, make sure to revise your materials to reflect that feedback, or any other information learned through the interview process. And again, don't necessarily expect a callback.

10

So You've Scored an Interview, Now What?

This chapter provides strategies for using a résumé and cover letter as a template to create talking points to make it through interviews and to prep references to speak on a law student's or young attorney's behalf. I will also share insights into dos and don'ts of interviewing for nonprofit and public interest positions, including strategies to speak to competencies and communicate shared values with a potential employer.

MAXIMIZING THE OPPORTUNITY TO INTERVIEW

Once you have submitted your materials and a potential employer has identified you as the preferred candidate, an employer may extend an invitation for you to interview. This will be an exciting point in the process because it means they like you. You may also be a bit nervous; this is also natural. The interview also represents your first opportunity to get directly in front of your audience and tell your story. When you receive an opportunity to interview, your next step is to continue to research the organization and team. You will not be expected to know in-the-weeds details about the organization and the role, but you should have a sense of the organization's mission and where the role you are applying for fits in. If you are applying to an organization with numerous offices across the state (or the country), you should be aware of the priorities of the office you are applying to. Your goal is to know as much about your potential employer as they know about you; achieving this helps you remain on brand through the interview process. Remember, know your audience.

TIP: AS YOU ARE DOING THIS SEARCH, ALWAYS BEGIN WITH THE "ABOUT" PAGE ON THE WEBSITE.

This page should discuss an organization's founding and mission. The website often also includes information about their mission, values, and practice areas. You should also be able to find information about staff members and members of the board. Use this information to develop questions for the interview. You can also look at a company's LinkedIn page to get a sense of their current programs, activities, and accomplishments. By looking at the "See all employees on LinkedIn" tab you can also learn about their individual roles and experiences with the organization.

Throughout the interview your goal is to demonstrate you are the preferred candidate. It is helpful to think of each interview as a conversation, as opposed to an interrogation. To this end, you should start the conversation with your interviewer if you are able. This can help you start with a short pitch and set the tone of the conversation. During conversation, you should demonstrate working knowledge of your résumé and try not to mention any new information or experience that is not detailed in your résumé or cover letter. In general, focusing on how your skills and experience equip you to make the organization and its work better is a safe strategy. You should also do your research.

Interviews are a two-way street, and you are interviewing an employer to see if the role and organization is a fit (i.e., aligns with your personal values, mission, and brand) just as much as they are interviewing you. You should use your research on the organization to craft questions to ask during the interview. As a rule of thumb, I encourage people to show up prepared with a minimum of three questions. Topics for these questions can range from expectations about the role to organizational culture. Asking questions that are relevant and thought-provoking can help make a solid impression on your interviewers and establish your brand as a personable, well-researched, preferred candidate.

ASSESSING WHETHER IT'S A MATCH

The vibe of an organization should become clearer as you get further along in the hiring process. Remember, you are also doing the interviewing, so it is important to know what to look out for along the way to see if the opportunity meets your expectations of organizational culture. Here are some questions that can help to guide you along the way:

1. Does the vibe and impression of the website match your interactions with staff?
2. Do you have a clear understanding of how the organization functions (and where you would fit in)?
3. Are there expectations beyond 9:00 am–5:00 pm?
4. Does the organization of the hiring process reflect the vibe and impression of the organization that you gained through research?
5. Does the energy of the interview match your expectations and vibe of the organization?

However, there are questions you should not ask in a first interview. Poorly formulated, run-of-the-mill questions may not leave a strong impression in any interview. You should also avoid asking about benefits, vacation, flexible scheduling, or other perks in the first interview; the only exception to this is if it is specifically prompted. You should also avoid overly focusing on training programs offered in a way that makes it seem self-serving or that you are only interested in a position because of what you could get out of it; organizations are interested in people who bring something to the table. Finally, you should be aware that if you are interviewing with multiple people they will share notes about you. Be clear and consistent in your answers. It is okay to say the same thing twice in different settings. This minimizes the risk of an interviewer taking a reworded answer out of context and sowing doubt as to your veracity or genuine interest in the organization or position.

It is true that interviews are a chance for an employer to get to know you. In this interview, it is a chance to showcase your personality and temperament. As you are engaging with the interviewers you should avoid pauses and be aware of your tone of voice. Be yourself, because the interviewers can tell when you are uncomfortable, nervous, inauthentic, or putting on a show. In the interview you should also be aware of body language and energy level, and try to make sure that yours matches that of the interviewer. For example, if an interviewer is fast-paced and upbeat, your responses should be similar, as long as it is authentic to you. Differing body language and energy level can throw off the dynamic of an interview. To this end, if you notice sustained differences in tone and energy throughout the interview process it may be an indication that the organization's culture may not be a fit. This may not be a dealbreaker for you, but you should be aware and ask questions to this end.

As the saying goes, opportunity is when luck meets preparation. Once you have become the preferred candidate, stay on brand and nail the interview.

YOUR FIRST INTERVIEW (AND ALMOST EVERY INTERVIEW THEREAFTER)

So far, this chapter has provided global feedback on interviews, but you may still have questions about what to expect and how to prepare. As a newly minted 1L, you will inevitably embark upon the illustrious search for that first internship. And after submitting a number of well-tailored applications, you will eventually be offered an opportunity to interview. Whether it is your first interview as a law student, or you have done a hundred interviews, you should always prepare. The first task is to research; you should always familiarize yourself with the organization, the position, and the bios of the people interviewing you. The second task is to review your materials and reflect. Self-awareness is a necessary trait when interviewing, as you should have evaluated your skills and interests against those the potential employer is seeking. To this end, there are questions you should be prepared to answer. These questions can include why you are interested in the position or organization and details about your experience. If you are employing my strategy, you should be doubly prepared to answer these questions because you "started with yourself" to clarify your mission and purpose.

Your next task is to prepare your questions for the interviewers. These questions should be informed by your research. I once came across a 1L who had recently been extended an invitation to their first interview. We were talking through what to expect in their interviews when they asked an astute question: *What questions are appropriate for a 1L to ask during an interview?* Her law school journey began after she spent a couple of years working after graduating college, so she had experience interviewing for jobs, but some of her go-to questions seemed inapplicable to her first law interview. If you are in this position during interview prep, do not fret. Here are some questions to consider:

- What is the structure of your internship program?
- What type of work will I be doing? Are there specific projects I would be working on?

- What does a day in the life of an intern at your organization look like?
- How will I receive feedback on my work?

These questions are a sampling of questions that are low stakes, succinct, and reflect the potential experience of an intern. Other questions you may ask are about colleague experience or about an interviewer's perspective on the organization's mission and work in furtherance of it. Regardless of where you land, questions should not be inappropriate or easily found through Google (indicating you have not done your research). If you are unsure of what to ask, brainstorm or vet your questions with a friend or mentor.

In preparation for your interview, you should also take advantage of the career services office at your law school. It is not often in life when you will have free experts at your fingertips. Not only can they review your materials, but they can likely also moot you; that is, offer a practice interview, or provide additional information on a particular opportunity. (Remember, you are not the first law student ever. It is likely that students who came before you worked in that same internship or same job.) There is no need to reinvent the wheel. And the preferred candidate will have a strategy that fully takes advantage of the resources available to them.

MAKE A GOOD FIRST IMPRESSION

Whether your interview is in person or virtual, you need to make a good impression on your employers. However, the way that you make a good impression will differ depending on the medium of the interview. The common ways to make a good first impression are through your actions, attitude, and appearance. If your interview is in person, show up early and be enthusiastic. When you enter the office, be sure to greet any staff you interact with, including secretarial and support staff. It is extremely common for people to provide informal feedback, so if you ignore the person who let you into the building you should assume that information will reach your interviewers. As you greet your potential future colleagues you should do your best to exude confidence; you can project confidence by proactively introducing yourself, having a firm handshake, and making eye contact. You should make sure you have a portfolio with copies of your résumé just in case your interviewers need one. It is also important to make sure your cell phone is turned off, set to either do not disturb or airplane mode, or that your phone settings are silent with no vibrating notifications.

Appearance is a loaded subject, laden with biases about what is "professional" attire. I will refrain from giving specific advice about dress; at this stage you have likely received more than enough advice about professional business attire (and if you haven't, a quick Google search should suffice). However, as you are getting dressed for your interview you should consider your brand and how you want to be remembered by your interviewers. You should do yourself a favor and not wear anything distracting. Your goal should be to be remembered by the interviewer(s) as the preferred candidate based on your experience and acumen. It will not serve your purpose if your interviewers remember you had on yellow glasses but don't remember anything else.

UTILIZING YOUR REFERENCES

For better or for worse, many jobs require you to provide references. As mentioned earlier, you should never waste precious space by including this information on your résumé. If an employer requires that references be submitted you should include them, uniformly formatted, in the body of the email where you have attached your materials to submit your application. If you are submitting your application through an online system, follow the instructions of that system. Regardless of how references are submitted, it is important to keep your references informed about the particular job and apprised of developments in the hiring process.

If you have made it to the stage of the hiring process where a company is asking for your references and they did not previously do so at the application stage, you are close to having the opportunity in the bag. In other words, it is often yours to lose. And reference checks are a freebie to make yourself look good to your future employer where the ball is truly in your court. Think about it. You have the opportunity to choose three references who know you, know your work, and can speak glowingly about both. You can also prep them in advance with talking points you want them to parrot. It is sometimes the case that an employer may want one of your references to come from a former supervisor, and if you have a good relationship, going this route, even if it is not required, may be a good strategy because of their familiarity with you. Applicants often think the most important characteristic about a reference is how well-known they are. However, it doesn't matter how famous someone is or how respected they are in the field if they cannot speak passionately and knowledgeably about you. If possible, you should try to include a current or former supervisor who can speak to your work. Do not squander the opportunity to seal the deal and back up your brand with a solid reference by relying on a recommender's stature instead of your relationship. This is especially true for recommendations by letter.

Letters of reference are a critical part of the application process for many public interest fellowships, and a great letter of recommendation can help your application stand out in a crowd. I have seen an awful recommendation from a U.S. senator on behalf of an applicant who interned with their office during the summer of law school. Similarly, another applicant's letter from a well-respected civil rights attorney did little to add to their candidacy because it did not include any evidence of familiarity. In both cases, it was abundantly clear that the referrers had little to no meaningful relationship with the applicants.

If an employer (or fellowship committee) would like to contact references by phone, make sure your references are *easily reachable by phone*. If a phone call is required, don't risk (or even delay) an opportunity because your references cannot be reached. Similarly, if references will be reached by email, be sure to inform them and give them a heads up that they will be contacted. It should go without saying, but whether you are asking someone to write a letter on your behalf or asking someone to serve on call as a reference for an employer, you should make sure they know you and can speak to your talents and experience. A poor reference can sink your candidacy just as quickly as a glowing one can propel it.

There are some positions that may sometimes require your list of references upfront (e.g., clerkships and some fellowships or positions using an applicant tracking system). Oftentimes, a potential employer will call the references that you have provided in order to verify your credentials. You should use your résumé and cover letter as a "cheat sheet" to prep your references (who you have informed in advance). When a reference agrees, send an email to confirm the details and thank them. This email should include your résumé, cover letter, talking points, and any other information a reference will need to know or that you would like them to be primed on to mention. You should always make serving as a reference as easy as possible. Do not forget to follow up with any outcomes and SAY THANK YOU.

RECEIVING THE OFFER

If you are lucky, after a long hiring and interview process you receive an offer. (Congratulations!) When you receive it, never accept it on the spot, even if it is your dream job. Whether the offer is made by email or over the phone, you should always confirm receipt of the offer and thank the employer. You should ask for more details on total compensation in writing, as well as for some time to evaluate it.

If you are interested and not going to decline the offer outright, it is important to always negotiate. And to best negotiate, you will need to do more research and give yourself an opportunity to reflect.

As you are reflecting, it is important to evaluate how this position relates to your long-term goals. Consider whether the position will allow you to hone the skills you have or develop new ones. If the position is an interim step, make sure you can articulate how this opportunity is a strategic next step to becoming the preferred candidate. It is also important for law students and young lawyers to assess the opportunity costs of the position, including what you will not be able to participate in or take advantage of if you take the position. Reflecting on these key questions can help you pause and check your opportunity against your goals and intent (as well as how feasible it is to take the position).

Once you have an offer, you should reflect on the following questions to determine whether this opportunity fits into your long-term strategy:

- Will this position allow me to continue to hone the skills I have?
- Will this position allow me to build the skills I seek to develop?
- Is this position a strategic step to becoming the preferred candidate?
- What opportunities can I not take advantage of by taking this position?
- What skills will I still need to acquire to be the preferred candidate?

Opportunity costs of professional opportunities are real, and depending on the opportunity those costs can be steep. For example, if a job is low paying, are you able to have a side hustle? Would you be required to relocate and, if so, is relocation assistance provided? Would taking this opportunity present conflicts of interest with other activities, such as boards you may serve on or organizations you volunteer with? These are just a sample of questions to consider when evaluating an opportunity, as a professional opportunity may have consequences of magnitude in terms of other aspects of your life. Most importantly, in addition to consulting with your mentor or other trusted advisors, you should also consider consulting your financial advisor to explore the financial implications before making such a decision.

11

Your Professional Future

It is my hope that this book can serve as a critical resource for law students and young attorneys looking to serve in the public's interest. However, it is never too late to get control of your career and either get back on track with your original interests or change the direction of your career, even if you are more than a few years post-law school. While this book includes tips and tricks, and dos and don'ts of résumé writing and interviewing, this is intended to be a long-term strategy and not a one-off self-help book. As you move through your career you will likely find that some advice is timeless; that is, the advice in this book may be relevant at many stages throughout your career, even though you may implement it differently. Accomplishing goals requires planning, determination, and intentional, consistent work. It is never too late to start with yourself and envision your future, build your brand and become the preferred candidate, and ensure that you remain competitive through annual skill building. This will be critical to maintaining and strengthening your brand and, thus, equipping you to remain competitive in the field over time.

Personal brand recognition and power can grow exponentially over time if that brand strategically invests in itself and associates itself with the "right" people, experiences, and other brands. It may be hard to believe at the outset, but the legal profession is small. You should expect to do a lot of networking: at conferences, CLEs, bar association events, and so on. Putting your best foot forward professionally, by its very nature, includes an on-brand résumé and cover letter, and personal, continuous follow-up that matches earlier impressions. The power of this strategy is its self-perpetuating nature, allowing law students and young attorneys to take the reins on their career.

THE POWER OF NETWORKS

There is no doubt that the legal field is a relational business, but law students and young attorneys should be careful not to place too much emphasis on network over personal brand and substance. Far too often people bank on getting an unmerited shot somewhere through the strength of networking. The assumption that access, or entitlement, to opportunity should come from who you know is often a symptom of an overly simplistic sense of what networking actually is that is based in rugged individualism and a consumption-based approach. From this perspective, networking is mostly about meeting the right people and getting as much as you can out of them for your own personal gain and benefit. Many people believe an opportunity should be given once they have simply met the right person and made an ask. Unfortunately, that is not how it works.

When it comes to accessing opportunities, a common refrain is that it is not what you know, but who you know. Working your network is often an important part of landing your ultimate dream position. In reality, there is more nuance to it. It is not enough to know people, even if they are the "right" people; you need to be in relationship with them. No one can go it alone, and you don't need to. In this field, you need to know who your crew is. In knowing your crew, you should know who has blazed or is blazing the path, who is coming alongside you, and who is coming up behind you. You never know when you will need help or guidance, or when someone may be in a position to make a decision that can change the direction of your career. Being in a relationship is important because your career is long and it is critical to build bridges, not burn them.

As a law student or young attorney, you should expect to ask for help. As you move along in your career you should expect to be asked. The relative lack of entry-level training programs means it is especially important to reach as you climb to continue to build a strong bench of diverse, mission-driven public interest attorneys. When you do so, I hope you pass along some of the knowledge gained through this approach.

12

Using This Advice to Thrive

This book contains a compendium of information to help law students and young attorneys, as well as lawyers looking to transition their careers, chart their course, and define their trajectory in the public interest. The core of the strategy consists of three steps. First, start with yourself and envision (in detail) the career you would like to have. Second, become the preferred candidate by strategically seeking opportunities to build the preferred skills listed on a position description of your dream job. Finally, demonstrate your growth and development by using your resume to showcase your skill acquisition and accomplishments in both your "day job" and your service to the profession and the community.

KEY TAKEAWAYS

- Your resume is the physical manifestation of your brand, so put your best foot forward. This means your materials should be solid in both substance and presentation.
- Use the opportunity of submitting a cover letter to tell your story. Remember, you should craft your résumé in a

compelling way to sell your experience and use your cover letter to bring your résumé to life with supporting details. Be sure not to waste space on your cover letter regurgitating your résumé.

- Know your audience. Knowing your audience will inform how you tailor your materials for the opportunity. When talking to your audience be sure to use plain English, avoid adjectives, and make every word count.
- Follow the instructions of the organization's process of submission. Whether you are submitting materials to a potential employer, applying to an award, or expressing interest in a board position, make sure to send your materials in the manner they prefer to receive them. And always try your best to address your submission to a specific person.
- Remember, stay on brand during your follow-up correspondence and interviews. First impressions are critical, but so is maintaining good relationships across the profession.

FINAL WORDS

My underlying motivation in writing this book is to equip future public interest attorneys with the tools to thrive in the public interest sector. It is my hope that this book is a tangible contribution toward inclusivity in the legal profession, especially for those who serve the public interest. What I endeavored to do in this book is provide the context necessary to tailor that advice and demystify the public interest sector, thereby helping law students and young attorneys launch their careers. The advice shared is also a look behind the curtain into public interest hiring. As such, there is something in this book for everyone. However, it isn't just providing advice, it provides law students and attorneys the tools to translate that advice into an executable strategy.

True to its name, this book provides advice to thrive by. My strategy is designed to empower you to create the plan to help you achieve your goals. Remember, goals are bigger then plans, which is why starting with yourself is so important. Dream big. Plan smart. And as you are employing this strategy, be sure to share the knowledge.

Appendix
Additional Resources

American Bar Association for Law Students, https://abaforlawstudents.com/.

Neil W. Hamilton, *Roadmap: The Law Student's Guide to Meaningful Employment,* 2 ed. (2018).

The National Archives and Records Administration, *The Federal Résumé Guide: What You Should Know When Applying for a Federal Career:* https://www.archives.gov/files/careers/jobs/forms/resume-guide.pdf (last accessed Feb. 24, 2022).

Richard Poulin, *Lawyer Resume Hacking: Shortcuts to Outshining Your Peers and Getting Interviews* (2015).

Shauna C. Bryce, *How to Get a Legal Job: A Guide for New Attorneys and Law School Students* (2012).

Wendy Enelow & Louise Kursmark, *Modernize Your Resume, Get Noticed … Get Hired,* 2 ed. (2016).

Yale Law School's Toolkit for Student Job Seekers, https://law.yale.edu/student-life/career-development/students/toolkit-student-job-seekers (last accessed Feb. 23, 2022).

About the Author

Portia Allen-Kyle is a civil rights attorney whose career has spanned government, academia, and the nonprofit sector in service to Black communities and communities of color. In 2021, she was recognized as one of the Top 40 lawyers under 40 by the American Bar Association. A dedicated mentor and sponsor of young attorneys, especially Black attorneys and attorneys of color, Portia is "building the bench" because she believes the generational pursuit of justice requires sustained investment in future advocates.

Portia has served as a presidential appointee in the Biden administration, serving as the Senior Advisor in the Departmental Office of Civil Rights at the US Department of Transportation. Before her federal service, she worked for nonprofits like the Council of State Governments Justice Center, the American Civil Liberties Union, and a start-up voting rights organization. Recognizing the intersection of policy and politics, she has served as a trusted campaign advisor, including as a policy advisor to the 2020 Democratic Primary Candidate Pete Buttigieg. Portia previously taught sociology and criminal justice courses at Rutgers University and St. Thomas Aquinas College. Other professional experiences include speaking and consulting on equity and social justice strategies across issues such as education, democracy, criminal justice, and organizational mission and alignment. Portia enjoys traveling, reading, live theater, and museums in her spare time. She earned her BA from Wellesley College, an MA in African-American Studies from Columbia University, an MA in Sociology from Rutgers University, and a JD from Rutgers University School of Law-Newark.

Index